YOU MUST REMEMBER THIS

ROBERT WAGNER is the star of such films as *A Kiss Before Dying*, *The Longest Day*, *The Pink Panther*, and most recently, the Austin Powers franchise. On television, he starred in *It Takes a Thief* (with Fred Astaire), *Switch* (with Eddie Albert and Sharon Gless), and *Hart to Hart* (with Stefanie Powers). He has recently appeared on *Two and a Half Men* and *NCIS*. He is married to actress Jill St. John and lives in Colorado and Los Angeles.

SCOTT EYMAN is the author of eleven books about the movies, including *Lion of Hollywood: The Life of Louis B. Mayer* (which the *Wall Street Journal* called one of the five best books ever written about Hollywood), *Empire of Dreams: The Epic Life of Cecil B. DeMille*, and most recently, *John Wayne: The Life and Legend*.

Praise for *You Must Remember This*

"In terms of grace and style, you couldn't ask for a better tour director than actor Robert Wagner. *You Must Remember This* is his valentine to the Hollywood he knew as a kid and enjoyed even more as a gape-worthy star in his own right. . . . Wagner writes with the easy charm he brought to the television series *Hart to Hart* and scores of movies and TV appearances. His amusing and interesting reflections carry a touch of wistfulness." —Associated Press

"In his new book, *You Must Remember This: Life and Style in Hollywood's Golden Age*, Wagner and his collaborator Scott Eyman offer a humorous, poignant, and sometimes juicy view of a vanished era. . . . His book talks about the legendary stars' grandiose mansions . . . and takes us inside the era's famed restaurants such as Chasen's (where Bob Hope once rode through the dining room on a horse) and the Brown Derby and the glittery nightclubs such as the Cocoanut Grove . . . and shows how the stars maintained their high style in everything they did, from their hobbies to their clothes." —*Los Angeles Times*

"[A] charming tribute to off-screen lives during a period many may regard as Hollywood's finest." —*Kirkus Reviews*

"[*You Must Remember This*] takes you into the palatial mansions, castles, and luxurious houses of the stars in great detail. It will become a great reference book for all lovers of silent and talkie movies and the actors and the actresses who peopled those homes. Fairbanks, Pickford, and Chaplin, they are all here amongst many others." —Ann McDonald, RedCarpetCrash.com

"With great affection and a twinkle in his eye, veteran actor Wagner recalls Hollywood's glory days of the 1940s and early 1950s, when class, manners, friendship, and a code of values ruled the city of stars. . . . An expert storyteller, Wagner entertains with tales of restaurants like the Brown Derby—where the Cobb salad was invented—the Trocadero, and the Mocambo, where elegance, entertainment, and great food filled a triple bill every night; in their day, restaurateurs such as Mike Romanoff and Dave Chasen were stars as big as Frank Sinatra and Bette Davis." —*Publishers Weekly*

"Wagner . . . paints a beautiful portrait of the glamorous places—restaurants, hotels, golf courses, and luxurious homes—that made Los Angeles the perfect playground for movie stars. He writes . . . lovingly of his many famous friends, as Fred Astaire, Clark Gable, Cary Grant, Elizabeth Taylor, Carole Lombard, and many more pass through his stories. . . . Wagner paints a lovely picture of an erstwhile era."
                                                        —*Parade*

"An affectionate new memoir . . . like a guided tour of vintage Hollywood."
                                                        —*Newsday*

"*You Must Remember This* . . . is like Wagner himself, wonderfully entertaining. . . . Any film fan will find much to enjoy."
                                                        —*The Buffalo News*

"Robert Wagner's true Hollywood stories go down easy, like the martinis at the Beverly Hills Hotel's Polo Lounge. . . . If Wagner had his own signature drink, it would be a mixture of elegance and enthusiasm—chased with charm. The closest thing to that concoction is his new book, *You Must Remember This: Life and Style in Hollywood's Golden Age*, a delightful tour of Wagner's memories of eight decades in Hollywood."
                                                        —*The Palm Beach Post*

Also by Robert J. Wagner

Pieces of My Heart (with Scott Eyman)

You Must Remember This

Life and Style in Hollywood's Golden Age

Robert J. Wagner

with Scott Eyman

A PLUME BOOK

PLUME
Published by the Penguin Group
Penguin Group (USA) LLC
375 Hudson Street
New York, New York 10014

USA | Canada | UK | Ireland | Australia | New Zealand | India | South Africa | China
penguin.com
A Penguin Random House Company

First published in the United States of America by Viking,
a member of Penguin Group (USA) LLC, 2014
First Plume Printing 2015

REGISTERED TRADEMARK—MARCA REGISTRADA

THE LIBRARY OF CONGRESS HAS CATALOGED THE VIKING EDITION AS FOLLOWS:
Wagner, Robert, 1930–
You must remember this : life and style in Hollywood's golden age / Robert J. Wagner with
Scott Eyman.
pages cm
Includes index.
ISBN 978-0-670-02609-8 (hc.)
ISBN 978-0-14-218194-2 (pbk.)
1. Wagner, Robert, 1930—Friends and associates.   2. Motion picture actors and
actresses—United States—Biography.   3. Motion picture producers and directors—
United States—Biography.   4. Motion picture industry—United States—History—
20th century.   I. Eyman, Scott, 1951–   II. Title.
PN2287.W235A3 20014
791.4302'8092—dc23
[B]
2013036970

Printed in the United States of America
10 9 8 7 6 5 4 3 2 1

Original hardcover design by Nancy Resnick

For my three daughters, Kate, Natasha, and Courtney,
who knew nothing about *This*.
For my grandson Riley and my granddaughter, Clover,
who knew nothing about *This*.
For my grandsons Cooper, Wyatt, and Theo,
who knew nothing about *This*.
And for my beautiful-in-every-way wife, Jill,
who knew something about *This*.

Contents

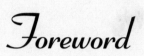

Foreword

first noticed that show business had gone crazy in 2002, when my
wife Jill St. John and I were guests at the wedding of Liza Minnelli and David Gest.

I had known Judy Garland, Liza's mother, since the very early fif-
ties, when she would sing at Clifton Webb's parties, backed up by
Roger Edens on the piano. I had been her escort to the royal premiere
in London of *I Could Go On Singing*, her last starring film. (And to
answer the obvious question, she was in very good shape that night—
thin and sober.) And Vincente Minnelli, Judy's ex-husband and Liza's
father, had shot a week or so of retakes for *All the Fine Young Canni-
bals*, a film I had made with my wife Natalie Wood at MGM in 1960.

As for David Gest, I had hosted all of the *Night of 100 Stars* pre-
sentations he had produced during the 1990s. In return, he had
made generous donations to the Motion Picture Home in Natalie's
name. For the *Night of 100 Stars* productions, which were backed by
Michael Jackson, David uncovered people who hadn't been seen for
decades: Turhan Bey, Clayton Moore, Silvia Sydney, Fay Wray, El-
eanor Powell, as well as stars of silent movies—archaeology combined
with showmanship. No one could have done it better than David.

The date of the wedding was March 16, 2002. The ceremony was scheduled for late afternoon, but we were all asked to be in black tie. I was sitting next to Robert Osborne, a close friend and the longtime host of Turner Classic Movies. All the guests were punctual, because David and Liza were determined that it wouldn't be one of those Hollywood weddings that start late. Even Michael Jackson was on time.

But Elizabeth Taylor, one of the two matrons of honor, was late. No surprise there. Elizabeth was always—and I do mean *always*—late. And once she finally did arrive, she realized that no one had brought the shoes she wanted to wear, so she sent someone back to the hotel on upper Fifth Avenue to fetch them. The church, needless to say, was on lower Fifth Avenue. Somewhere in the middle, a parade was taking place.

So we sat there.

Twenty minutes, and we still sat there. A half hour, and we sat there.

After a while people stopped looking at their watches. And we sat some more.

There really wasn't anything to do but look around the church. "We" included Donald Trump, Mickey Rooney, Tito Jackson (co–best man, along with Michael), Gina Lollobrigida, Lauren Bacall, Natalie Cole, Mia Farrow, Cindy Adams, Martha Stewart, Liz Smith, and 842 more of David and Liza's most intimate friends.

Bob Osborne and I discussed whether Liza had ever met Gina Lollobrigida before her wedding day. We decided it was highly doubtful.

Now, I have always had the greatest affection for Elizabeth. I first met her in the late 1940s at a party thrown by Roddy McDowall, her best friend for life. Everything that people say about Elizabeth's looks was truth: she was just illegally beautiful. Years later, Elizabeth and I had a fling, and years after that, I produced and costarred in a movie with her, *There Must Be a Pony*, based on James Kirkwood Jr.'s fictionalized memoir of his mother, the silent star Lila Lee.

I've always believed that Elizabeth was a terribly underrated actress, and I've always known that she was among the most generous people alive—not just with money, but with the most valuable commodity any of us possesses: her time.

But Elizabeth had her flaws as we all do. Foremost among them was that she was oblivious to the concept of punctuality. A delay of one or two hours was normal for people waiting for Elizabeth. I've always wondered whether it was a passive-aggressive way of asserting herself for all those years of enforced punctuality at MGM. But she was never late on our picture.

Unless she really, really liked you, Elizabeth was always late. And sometimes she was incredibly late even if she did like you. So I wasn't terribly shocked when, even after the gofer arrived back at the church with the correct shoes, we were still sitting there.

David Gest was growing noticeably perturbed, so he asked Michael Jackson to go find Elizabeth and bring her back alive. Neither David nor Liza wanted to personally force the issue, since they were so pleased that Elizabeth had agreed to come in the first place. Elizabeth was going through one of her bad phases—overweight and not looking good.

Michael disappeared into the room where Elizabeth was supposedly getting ready, while one of his bodyguards stood watch outside.

And then we waited some more.

By now the wedding was an hour late and counting.

I asked a man what the holdup was, but he just shrugged and said that Elizabeth was in a room with Michael Jackson.

Nobody seemed to be moving, and nobody seemed eager to break up whatever was going on in the waiting room. Because I knew Elizabeth so well, I was finally deputized to get Michael away from her so the wedding could proceed. Otherwise we all might find ourselves growing old, very slowly, at the Marble Collegiate Church.

I walked past the bodyguard and into the room.

Elizabeth was sitting there, gazing at Michael. Michael was on his knees, gazing at Elizabeth. He was holding her hand. Nothing was being said. He was besotted with her; he was drinking her in.

"Michael," I said, "we have to get the wedding started. We *have* to get going."

"I want to be with Elizabeth," Michael said in that weird, whispery voice. "I *love* Elizabeth."

Talking to Michael when he was in one of his reveries was exactly like talking to a six-year-old waiting up for Santa Claus: you didn't want to disabuse him of his fantasy, but you had to firmly lead him away from the Christmas tree so that the presents could be put out.

"I love her, too, Michael," I said. "We all love her. But we have to go ahead with the wedding. There's a church full of people out there, and they're getting restless. You can spend all the time you want with Elizabeth after the wedding."

Full disclosure: I was angry, so I might have said all this a little . . . brusquely. By this time I was heartily sick of the wedding, even though it hadn't even taken place yet. What I wanted to do was have a drink with Bob Osborne and not be bothered by infantile bullshit.

I got them moving, but Elizabeth came out on the wrong side of the church—the guests were divided into men on the left and women on the right—and so she had to walk all the way around behind the pews. Since Elizabeth was fairly immobile and walked with difficulty—part of it was her back, part of it was the medication for her back, which always gave her a buzz—she had to be helped onto the altar.

Finally—*finally*—the wedding got under way. David gave Liza a 3.5-karat diamond ring from Tiffany's. After the minister said he could kiss the bride, David tried to suck the lips off Liza's face. I was too appalled to say anything. Jill said, "*Ewww.*" Next to her, Liz Smith said, "Double *ewwww.*"

The reception afterward was huge. Andy Williams sang. Gloria Gaynor sang. Michael Jackson gave the toast. I noticed some people I hadn't noticed at the wedding: Kirk Douglas, Joan Collins, and Sid Luft, one of Liza's stepfathers. Elizabeth skipped the reception. I finally had my drink with Bob Osborne.

For a long time after that, David would call Jill and me to chat. "You two are the happiest people I know," he would begin, "and now I've found the same thing. I'm so in love with her. I go to bed with her and I rest my head on her right breast." Then Liza would come on the line and tell me how wonderful David was, and that she was finally, unbelievably happy. They were nuts about each other.

They divorced in 2007. It was, needless to say, acrimonious. For a while David lived in England; now I understand that he's in Nashville.

That was the day I began to think seriously about the business in which I have spent my life. Ever since then, I've felt that while the wedding was not exactly a Fellini movie, it was close.

And it was then that I began thinking about how show business had changed.

Now, Judy Garland's marriage to Vincente Minnelli was probably no more plausible than Liza's to David Gest. But the difference is that the former was designed and directed by MGM so as to minimize damage to the reputations of a major star and a major director. The full extent of the emotional, psychological, and sexual misalliance between Judy and Vincente didn't become apparent until years later, after they had left the protective shelter of the studio.

It needs to be pointed out that David was in many respects very good for Liza. He got her thin; he got her performing again and her career has continued at a stellar level. But Liza's way with men derives from her mother's. She's neurotic and she's beguiling. She would put her life in someone's hands and convince him that he was the only one who could possibly save her. At some point, either David became too exhausted to carry on or the intrinsic problems in the relationship reared up and destroyed the marriage.

Eleven years after that wedding, things are . . . even more bizarre. Recently I was idly watching TV when a formerly thin actress who'd become fat, then thin and back again in what is apparently an endlessly recurring cycle, showed up to promote a reality show. Since she's now fat, nobody hires her to act, because there aren't a lot of parts for middle-aged fat women, movies and TV being predominantly a medium of fantasy.

So her only means of making a living is appearing as a formerly thin actress grown fat who is trying to get thin again.

I turned to Jill and asked a question: "This is a career?"

I didn't really expect an answer, which is good, because I didn't get one. Some questions don't have answers. And I'm compelled to admit that being a fat actress and playing oneself is not really a bad gig. If nothing else, she's working. Intermittently, but still, she's working.

All this got me thinking about the quantum differences between now and then—then being right after World War II, when I got into the movies. And it got me thinking not just about the movies themselves, but about the differences in Hollywood, the town I've been a part of for seventy-five years.

On the most basic level, the difference is 180 degrees. For instance, when I worked on *The Longest Day* for Darryl Zanuck, he commanded a huge force of actors and extras, and the film was shot on the actual locations, at Omaha Beach and so forth.

Darryl organized his version of the D-day landing by flying green flags for "Attack," yellow flags for "Caution," and red flags for "Stop." I was in the sequence about rappelling up Pointe du Hoc, and we shot it at Pointe du Hoc, doing it exactly the way the American soldiers had done it less than twenty years before.

Today when a battle scene is mounted, the extra call is greatly diminished, and the body count and the effects are completed and amplified through the oddly weightless effects of computer-generated images (CGI). Through some inverted math, the numbers of the combatants are incalculably greater, but the effect is halved, because you don't really believe what you're seeing. The pervasive lack of reality of so much modern filmmaking has made spectacle less spectacular.

Back then, we worked a six-day week, there was no such thing as overtime, and the large board at the studio that contained the shooting schedule for each picture on the lot was rarely altered—if Darryl wanted a movie made in forty days and you fell a little behind, then you could confidently expect to be pulling an all-nighter on that fortieth day because it would, by God, be done in the allotted time.

When I started out, I worked in front of a camera filled with film, and each take was signaled by the *slap!* of a clapper board, which was used to synch the sound. Today, the cameras are all digital, with no gentle but comforting *whirrr* of the camera, and the "clapper board" offers only a digital readout.

And I can assure you that if an actress got too fat at Darryl Zanuck's place of business—or, for that matter, Jack Warner's or Louis B. Mayer's—the studio would not have dropped her any faster than if she had contracted a venereal disease and infected half the studio.

Certain things weren't done, and fat was one of them. Nor were there a lot of alternatives to the movies. TV was further down the food chain, with less money and less prestige, although that began to change in the 1960s.

In the golden days of Hollywood, stars didn't have much, if any, say over the parts we played, or, for that matter, over what movies we made. In fact, even famous executives like Zanuck and Mayer weren't truly autonomous—Hollywood always had a way of answering to New York on matters of budget and overall policy.

Following this train of thought, I've realized that people in the movie industry, whether actors, directors, or producers, used to exercise real control only over their private lives. But even then things could be heavily monitored, as Judy Garland found out.

And all this is what has brought me to this book about the quantum differences between then and now, as seen in how we lived our private lives during the last gasp of radiance that was the studio system. I want to try to document a way of life that has vanished as surely as birch bark canoes. And I want to do this before the colors fade.

It cannot be overemphasized that the movie industry of the late 1940s was a family business. Jack and Harry Warner were running Warner Bros. just as they had been since World War I; Harry Cohn was running Columbia just as he had since shortly after that war; Louis B. Mayer was running MGM just as he had since the company was formed in 1924.

These men knew one another intimately, distrusted one another greatly, competed against one another constantly. They engaged in the kind of bitter squabbles and fights—at times physical—that can be understood only as family quarrels. Eventually, these men were squeezed out—by time, by death, once or twice by each other. I think it's fair to say that, at least at Hollywood's beginnings, they were too busy to really be conscious of what they were building, but they certainly believed in themselves, so they built something that has lasted. More important, they made movies that will undoubtedly outlast the studios that financed them.

For all their at times petty vindictiveness, those brawling, hostile, often ill-educated men stood behind the movies that came from their studios in a way that the far more educated and sophisticated people who run the studios today don't. Warner and Cohn, Mayer and Zukor, Goldwyn and the rest made movies they genuinely believed in; they made movies they wanted to see themselves. They took pride in the product.

For them, their work was intensely personal—a reflection of their dreams and aspirations.

The Harvard MBAs who run the multinational corporations who own the studios today don't make movies for themselves. They make movies for an audience they don't know and probably don't want to know. They might be proud of their quarterly earnings, but, in most cases, they can't possibly be proud of their movies.

And while I'm on the subject, let me just say that the importance placed on constantly improving corporate earnings is one of the worst things to happen to the movie industry, and quite possibly to America. It turns the attention of the public and the industry away from the quality of the pictures to the amount of money a picture or a company can make. In this way the movie business has been converted from a long game into a short game. At the same time, the multinational corporations that own movie studios seem to do it more out of corporate vanity than anything else, because a hit movie doesn't really move the needle of their stock price—it's like punching a blanket. If Zanuck had a hit, the stock price and the dividends both went up.

Darryl Zanuck and Jack Warner played it both ways, but when pressed to the wall, they played the long game. Darryl knew *The*

Grapes of Wrath was not going to be a huge moneymaker, but he didn't care. It wasn't very expensive to produce, it would make money over time, and it would accrue prestige to the studio and the industry that made it.

And Darryl was right. *The Grapes of Wrath* broke even in 1940, and it has never stopped playing in more than seventy years.

I suspect that for the men and women who run studios today, it's just a business. But for Warner, Zanuck, and the rest of them, it was a passionate pursuit—they had a vision they wanted to put on-screen, and Hollywood grew around that vision.

I guess you might say that *You Must Remember This* is my farewell to the lives that those of us lucky enough to be in the movie industry lived.

While the book is partly about style and status, I hope that it will also offer an intimate look at people and what they were like away from the studio and publicity machine—stars and filmmakers at home, entertaining, having dinner with friends. Some of the book will be about the stars I knew best, from the homegrown American variety (Gary Cooper, Clark Gable), to the British colony (Cary Grant, David Niven), to Americans who imitated the British colony (Douglas Fairbanks Jr.). Other parts of the book will be about our houses, the architects who built them, the haberdashers who dressed us, the restaurants where we liked to eat and why. It will be about the way Hollywood actually lived, told via a mosaic of memory.

I will trace the changing times and styles that I've lived through. For instance: For about twenty years, William Haines, once the only out-of-the-closet actor at MGM, was probably the preeminent decorator to the stars. After he got cashiered by Metro—it didn't pay to flaunt homosexuality around Louis B. Mayer—Haines decorated a house for his friend Joan Crawford.

Then Billy bought a house on North Stanley Avenue in Hollywood and decorated it in a combination of colonial New Orleans and eighteenth-century English. The story goes that Irving Thalberg came to visit the house and, as Haines showed him around, kept asking, "Who did this?"

"I did," Billy replied each time. Word got around, and Billy went into the interior decoration business and did extremely well.

The style that Billy evolved—white or bright fabrics, clean surfaces—began to go out of fashion in the 1950s. He still got decorating jobs, many from his friends in the Old Guard—he did a lot of decorating for the Reagans and their circle—but younger people wanted their own decorators, their own look. They always do. New designers came in, and styles changed.

Watching the ebb and flow of fashion in the microcosm of Los Angeles and its related towns, I've developed a sense of time as a river, always moving, always shifting the outlines of the banks. I see Los Angeles as a mutable organism—it never quite looks the same way twice. I remember a town of Red Car trolley lines and weekends spent at Catalina playing baseball with John Wayne and John Ford.

Gone, all gone.

This is a book about life outside the studio walls, from the very beginnings of Hollywood, to when I got there in the 1930s, through the 1950s and 1960s—a window into a bygone world of splendid glamour that can, for most, be experienced only vicariously.

My intent is for you to experience the same thrill I did, one night at Clifton Webb's house. It was a dinner party, thrown with all of Clifton's impeccable taste. And then it became something more. Roger Edens, the associate producer for the Arthur Freed unit at MGM, began to play the piano and Judy Garland got up to sing for the better part of an hour—Gershwin, Porter, Harry Warren.

While she serenaded us with that great golden trumpet of a voice, Clifton's small poodles wandered around the room as dogs do, looking for food or affection.

I also saw Judy sing at the Palace in New York, but this was like nothing else. Watching her sing to a crowded theater paled in comparison to being in a room with her by the piano and fifteen people gathered around. There was a palpable, intimate quality that was unforgettable, and it was a complete thrill that I've never forgotten.

We who were lucky enough to be in the movie industry at that time lived in a cocoon of golden lace. We were protected from the consequences of our behavior by the vast studio apparatus and by a comprehensively different public attitude. We had freedom and, frankly, most of the time we also had license.

If there was an arrest for drunk driving, there would be a nod, a wink, perhaps some modest amount of money changing hands, and that would be the end of it. No police record, let alone a trial. If an actor behaved the way that, say, Tiger Woods did—and believe me, it was not unusual—it was covered up. No one knew, and no one would ever know . . . except fixers at the studio.

No more. Now one of the prime ways to get on the cover of a magazine or to juice up a career is to go into rehab for alcohol or drugs, have a public psychotic episode, or make a porn tape. Even something as commonplace as a woman getting out of a car can be used to whip up a frenzy, if it's done sans underwear.

Then, stars could move around town more or less at will. We shopped for our own clothes during regular business hours, we often bought our own groceries, and we flew commercial. And when we flew commercial, we dressed up—maybe not in a tie, but at the very least we always wore a jacket. Wherever you were, there was rarely a sense of anything approaching hostility from the public, much less danger.

Now, the twenty-four/seven news cycle, with its hundred different news outlets, restricts behavior and enforces consequences. Brad Pitt and Angelina Jolie can't leave the house without a security detail hovering; if they have to go to the store they go after regular hours, and private airplanes are mandatory. The freedom that used to be one of the perks of celebrity is now virtually nonexistent—the size of the media lens is so much larger, and the focus is less forgiving. There are hordes of cameras, and anyone with a cell phone is a potential paparazzo. And stars can be brutalized by a media that has no filter, only stories—a lot of them manifestly untrue.

My sense is that today's celebrities trade the huge amounts of money they earn for an almost complete loss of freedom. The focus of the media is very close, and the view is totally unforgiving. And you know something? They can have it; I don't want it.

So this book is a loving farewell letter to the glorified mom-and-pop business I was lucky enough to get into. I've been so fortunate—my career has been going strong for more than sixty years, from Darryl Zanuck to *The Pink Panther* to *Hart to Hart*, from *Austin Powers* to *Two and a Half Men* and *NCIS*. That experience, that long view, enables me to examine how the values and motivations of moviemaking have changed.

But at the same time, some things never change. Then or now, Hollywood is about basic human drives: ambition, respect, the desire to be noticed, the need to be loved.

The nightclubs, some of the houses, and almost all of the people that I'll be telling you about are gone, as are the styles and fashions. But the movies and the legends remain, and the documenting of those places, of the way we lived, will trace the road between then and now.

The time I'm writing about was better than ours in some ways, and worse in others. I'll point up these behavioral and sociological differences as they occur. I hope this book will be like a good movie: a little spectacle, some laughs, a sense of reflection, all of it underlying an emotional authenticity.

Here is Hollywood as I knew it.

The Land

Before it became the world center for the production of entertainment and art, Los Angeles was just the end of the line. When you got there, you had gone as far as you could go.

It was an exotic place, and for a very long time it was also a bit unreal. Maybe it still is; I've been here so long—more than seventy-five years—that it just seems normal to me. But if you go back to the beginning, it was a place of open spaces and dreams that took a long, long time to come to fruition.

Before the movies, people came to Hollywood for the same reason they went to Florida: the weather. And before smog created temperature inversion, the weather was indeed glorious—seldom over 85 degrees in the hottest summer, rarely below 40 degrees in the coldest winter.

Hollywood was founded in the 1880s by Methodists from the Midwest who saw it as a place where temperance could flourish. First they banned liquor. A few years later, they banned movies.

Neither ban succeeded, thank God.

But everybody who came to Southern California then came to Los Angeles, not Hollywood. The population of Los Angeles skyrocketed from eleven thousand people in 1880 to fifty thousand ten years later, making it the fastest-growing city in the country. All that land west of Los Angeles was bound to become desirable, but when?

Developers appeared early. One of them was Horace Wilcox, who arrived from Kansas in 1883. Wilcox was a devout Methodist who had made a fortune in real estate and helped make Kansas safe for Prohibition.

Wilcox built a gabled Queen Anne house on a dirt road that he modestly named Wilcox Avenue, in a town that his wife named "Hollywood" after the name of a friend's estate in Ohio that she thought would work well for an entire town. Daeida Wilcox wanted Hollywood to be at the leading edge of the Temperance movement, a model of virtue that would set Christian soldiers marching as to war.

Wilcox offered free land to anybody who wanted to build a church. There were no saloons or liquor stores, no red-light district, and, above all, no theater people. The sign that was most frequently displayed read "No Jews, actors or dogs allowed."

I don't know about the dogs, but the Jews and actors were not easily discouraged. They bided their time.

As a temperance venture, Hollywood has to be considered a huge failure; as a real estate venture, an equally huge success.

Horace Wilcox died in 1890, and Hollywood was incorporated in 1903. In between those years, not a lot happened, aside, perhaps, from the construction of the Hollywood Hotel in 1903. Built along a Hollywood Boulevard that was then still a dirt road, the hotel was an old frame barn, part Moorish, part Spanish. It cost twenty-five thousand dollars, had thirty-three rooms, a bathroom on every floor, and a garden on the roof.

Sometime during World War II, I walked onto the veranda of the Hollywood Hotel and saw D. W. Griffith sitting in one of its rocking chairs, quietly surveying the town that he had done so much to build. Just a few years later, both Griffith and the hotel were gone.

The development of the modern Hollywood was an incremental process. A few highlights from its early history:

1904: Sunset Boulevard is completed from downtown Los Angeles to Laurel Canyon.

1905: Hollywood Cash Grocery, the very first store, opens on Cahuenga and Sunset.

1905: A trolley car begins running between Los Angeles and Hollywood every fifteen minutes.

A few places still survive from that era, although they're not in Hollywood proper but in Los Angeles. There's Olvera Street, which dates from the founding of the town. Then there's a restaurant with the delightful name Philippe the Original, which opened in 1908 on North Alameda Street and became famous for its French dip sandwiches served in a rustic atmosphere. It's still offering them, among other dishes. And the Pantry Café, which opened a little later, in 1924, on South Figueroa, is also still in business.

One of the early landmarks from that period was a mansion built by the artist Paul de Longpré in 1902 on three and a half acres on the corner of Hollywood and Cahuenga Boulevards. De Longpré was a mostly unsuccessful artist in France and New York who got that prime plot of real estate by bartering three original oil paintings for it. He proceeded to build a Moorish-style mansion and surround it with a spectacular Monet-style garden: five hundred rose bushes, a thousand tulip bulbs, jonquils, and fifty blooming trees. His skills as an artist paled next to his skills as a promoter; the public was invited to saunter through his home and garden. If they bought a painting or two en route, so much the better.

De Longpré's house was the first famous Hollywood mansion, and you might say that he also invented the modern American tourist attraction, which also functions as a glorified souvenir stand.

And while de Longpré's home is not among them, there are a number of hardy early-twentieth-century Hollywood survivors. (I'm partial to hardy survivors.) The Magic Castle, a Franklin Avenue landmark for decades as a place where magicians go to amuse other magicians, was built as a private home for a man named Rollin B. Lane in 1909. Yamashiro, a Japanese restaurant in the Hollywood Hills, was originally built in 1914 as a home by the Bernheimer family, leading New York importers of East Asian goods. They probably figured the house would be on the decorative leading edge, although the style never quite caught on, at least not in LA. After the stock market crash of 1929, the house passed through several hands until it was resurrected as a restaurant in 1949. All told, the buildings and the beautifully landscaped grounds have been Hollywood landmarks for a hundred years.

By 1911 Hollywood had banned anything that might lower the tone of the town: slaughterhouses were forbidden, as were gasworks, textile mills, and cotton fields. Why cotton fields? Because they required people—usually migrants—to pick the cotton; in addition to Jews, actors, and dogs, migrants were also unwelcome.

What flourished in Hollywood was not tolerance, but nature. Franklin Avenue was wreathed in pepper trees; Vine Street was covered in peppers and palms. Snaking through the hills but stopping far short of the ocean, Sunset Boulevard had a bridle path that ran right down its center. This made perfect sense, because a lot more people were getting around via horseback than via automobiles.

Between 1903 and 1910, Hollywood's population gradually increased—from seven hundred in 1903 to four thousand in 1910—but the character of its people remained the same. They were middle-class families who wanted to get away from cold weather and alcohol. Among the things that the board of trustees banned were the sale of liquor, gambling, and "disorderly houses"—i.e., whorehouses. As for pool halls and bowling alleys, they had to be closed by eleven p.m. on weekdays and all day on Sunday.

Other laws prohibited driving herds of more than two hundred horses, cattle, or mules, or more than two thousand sheep, through the streets. All that was official; still unofficially prohibited were actors, who couldn't find rooms to rent.

Things finally began to change when Cecil B. DeMille set up shop in December 1913 at a barn on the southeast corner of Selma and Vine in the heart of Hollywood. He was representing a consortium in New York that included Jesse L. Lasky and Samuel Goldwyn.

The Jesse L. Lasky Feature Play Company was not the first movie company to have offices in Southern California, but it was the first to establish year-round headquarters; the others were seasonal operations sent out by East Coast studios that were trying to maintain production during the impossible New York winters.

DeMille hadn't intended to end up in Hollywood; his original destination had been Flagstaff, but finding that he hated the light and the flat terrain in Arizona, he went on to the end of the line. Scanning the horizon for a likely place to set up a motion picture studio, he ended up at a barn owned by a man named Jacob Stern.

Members of the Famous Players–Lasky Corporation, which eventually became Paramount. From left to right: Jesse L. Lasky, Adolph Zukor, Samuel Goldwyn, Cecil B. DeMille, and Al Kaufman. In the end these men created more than Paramount—they created Hollywood.

A deal was struck, and DeMille erected a sign over the barn: JESSE L. LASKY FEATURE PLAY COMPANY. DeMille started shooting his first picture, *The Squaw Man*.

It was a western, and it was a smash hit. DeMille had lucked into something big. As he ramped up production, he found that the area could serve as background for almost every kind of movie, from desert—about eighty miles outside of Los Angeles—to mountains—fifteen minutes from DeMille's studio door.

Other studios noted the variety of locations. The gold rush was on.

I have a holster that was used in *The Squaw Man*, given to me by a wonderful man in the Fox still department who had worked on the picture. When I got into the movie industry in 1949, *The Squaw Man* was only thirty-five years old, or about as old as *The Deer Hunter* is now—lots of people who had been there with DeMille were still working, as was DeMille himself. The holster is one of those six-degrees-of-separation objects—a perfectly ordinary piece of leather that is also a piece of Hollywood history.

For the first few years of the Jesse L. Lasky Feature Play Company, Lasky himself commuted from New York and basically left production matters in the hands of his partner DeMille. But in 1917 Lasky bought a Spanish mansion at 7209 Hillside, right where La Brea dead-ends into the Hollywood Hills. The Lasky house's most exotic feature was a screening room—one of the first private screening rooms in Hollywood—along with the already standard tennis court and swimming pool. Lasky wouldn't have needed more than five minutes to get to the studio.

By 1915, the annual payroll of the studios in Hollywood totaled about twenty million dollars. By 1920 the population had grown to thirty-six thousand, and the new settlers were no longer teetotaling Midwesterners, but young men and women lured by the siren call of the movies.

There were still very few mansions in Hollywood, and hardly anything at all west of the town. Most of the aspiring actors and actresses, not to mention the writers and directors, rented hotel rooms or modest frame houses, if only because everyone was uncertain how long this movie thing was going to last and they didn't want to overextend themselves only to be brought up short by the sudden death of the fad.

In those early years, people seemed to want to stay close to the studios, if only to keep the commute short. There were exceptions;

around World War I, the most fashionable address in Los Angeles—
at least between Western Avenue and South Figueroa Street—
wasn't in Hollywood at all, but on West Adams Boulevard. Theda
Bara lived there for a while, just around the corner from the extremely rich oilman Edward Doheny.

After a time Theda Bara moved out, and Fatty Arbuckle moved
in. This was even worse. Bara was at least an actress, but Arbuckle
had worked for the lowly Keystone company. He was . . . *a comedian!* He was making five thousand dollars a week, but he was
still—*a comedian!*

Arbuckle was living at his West Adams home in 1921 when the
scandal erupted that destroyed his career and his life. He had thrown
a party in San Francisco's St. Francis Hotel, after which a girl named
Virginia Rappe died. Arbuckle was accused of manslaughter; there
were allegations of rape as well, although nobody who knew Arbuckle thought he was capable of committing rape. After a few trials
resulted in hung juries, he was acquitted, but he was banned from
the screen by newly hired morality czar Will Hays anyway. Arbuckle
sold the house to his boss—and later my boss—Joe Schenck.

Agnes de Mille would describe Hollywood at that point in its
history as "very lovely and romantic and attractive. . . . The streets
ran right into the foothills and the foothills went straight up into
sage brush and you were in the wild, wild hills. Sage brush and
rattlesnakes and coyotes and the little wild deer that came down
every night. And all of it was just enchanting."

Los Angeles didn't have traditions of its own, so it borrowed the
older traditions of California, a place of Spanish haciendas and

missions and a sense of leisure. In good times and bad, one thing stayed constant in California: a feeling for light and the ways in which the land could be made a part of the interior of the homes. The houses were Andalusian or Moorish, Italian or Spanish, but almost all of them were in some way romantic—the basis for Los Angeles, as well as for the movies.

In those early days, Beverly Hills landscaping was in the hands of the Englishman John J. Reeves, who wanted a different kind of tree for each street, all trimmed to uniform heights and widths. Reeves specified pepper trees for Crescent Drive, just south of the future site of the Beverly Hills Hotel. J. Stanley Anderson, whose grandmother managed the Beverly Hills Hotel, told me that some of the developers thought that maybe pepper trees weren't such a great idea, but Reeves insisted. He planted saplings, and they all blew down in the first storm, whereupon he was told to plant something sturdier.

"You are going to have peppers," replied the stubborn Mr. Reeves. So the pepper trees were replanted and stood for decades, until they died off and were replaced with Southern magnolias. By that time, Mr. Reeves was dead and could no longer bulldoze his way through obstacles.

All this care and planning yielded . . . nothing much.

But they still kept planning, confident that if they just kept building, sooner or later the world would come. Los Angeles was the fastest-growing city in America, so some of that had to benefit Hollywood and Beverly Hills, which was right next door. In the early part of February 1911, Margaret Anderson and her son Stanley Anderson were invited to own and operate a luxury hotel. Margaret had another grandson named Robert, but years later I became very good friends with J. Stanley Anderson, who told me many stories of early Hollywood.

Everything exploded outward in the 1920s.

The first fortunes of Southern California were created by oil, agriculture, railroads, and real estate. In Beverly Hills, real estate and natural resources were closely intertwined. (Real estate is still a driver of the local economy.) About this time, 80-by-165-foot lots were going for $1,100—the rough equivalent of $26,000 today, which just goes to show you that scarcity and location have more to do with the value of a piece of land than inflation.

The Depression affected Hollywood in a different way and at a different speed than it did the rest of the country. While most other cities were already in terrible shape by 1930, Hollywood didn't experience the full extent of the Depression until 1932 or so. Paramount went into receivership, RKO teetered, and Warner Bros. lost most of the money it had made in the early days of sound.

But by 1937, the year my family moved to Bel Air, the tide had turned. The town was once again beginning to hum, not just because of the quality of the movies being made, but because the studios manufactured one of the few means of escape for a world that was still struggling with the effects of the crash. And so Hollywood created an alternate reality—a collective fantasy, if you will—for a world where reality itself was ugly and unmanageable.

In 1937 MGM made forty-seven pictures, nearly one per week, while Universal came close to that, with forty-four movies—both amazing numbers. Yet Warner Bros. went far past them both, with sixty-six pictures. Hollywood was truly a factory, churning out movies the same way Ford churned out Model A's. A lot of these movies were low-budget B's, produced to fill the bottom of the double features that the studios had devised as a means of combating the economic downturn: two pictures for the price of one, with a dish giveaway in between them.

I first started going to the movies at the Carthay Circle in the Wilshire district almost from the day we started unpacking. I distinctly remember seeing Walt Disney's *Snow White and the Seven Dwarfs* there—the grassy divider in the middle of San Vicente Boulevard, which ran in front of the theater, featured three- and four-foot-high figures of all the dwarfs.

In those days LA was a movie town to an extent that's hard to imagine today. There was a big shipping business down by the docks in San Pedro and Long Beach—the second-largest port in the United States—but the driver of the local economy was primarily the movie business. In a few years World War II would change all that by propelling the airplane industry into prominence and broadening the economic base. Very quickly 750,000 people were working in the airplane business.

In 1937 I was seven years old, a kid from the Midwest—Detroit, to be specific. I was just beginning my love affair with the movies, which I was lucky enough to parlay into a career.

My father was a brilliant businessman. He made a great deal of money in the 1920s selling the lacquer that was used on the dashboards of Fords, then lost it all in the stock market crash and the Depression, when nobody had any money to buy new cars.

But by the latter part of the thirties, he had recovered enough capital to make the move to the West Coast, which had been recommended for my mother's asthma. At the time, most of the movie people still lived in Hollywood or Beverly Hills; Bel Air was thinly settled at that point, but that's where my father chose to live. I believe he paid twenty thousand or thirty thousand dollars for a lot, and around forty thousand dollars to build a house there. I'm not sure if there was a surcharge to construct the street to access it, but it was in any event as new as our house on 10887 Chalon Road.

The house is still standing, and, with the help of a great many people, so am I.

Our home had three bedrooms; next to it was a pool and a guesthouse. It was Spanish in style, and had a hitching post in the backyard for the horses we were expected to have, and did. We didn't keep them at the house, but at the stables at the Hotel Bel Air when it finally opened in 1946.

I immediately loved California, the way each block offered something delicious for the eye. Compared to suburban Detroit, it was intoxicating. Not everybody, though, was enthralled with the prevailing mode of architecture and decoration. Nathanael West wrote about the environment in *The Day of the Locust*: "Only dynamite would be of any use against the Mexican ranch houses, Samoan huts, Mediterranean villas, Egyptian and Japanese temples, Swiss chalets, Tudor cottages and every possible combination of these styles."

West was a good writer, but I didn't share his feelings—not then, not now. Los Angeles, like the industry it spawned, was first about creating desire, then satisfying it—a profoundly American gift.

Bel Air had been opened to development by a man named Alphonzo Bell in 1922. And yes, at first there was a strict policy that forbade selling to movie people, which I find ironic. It seems that Bell wanted his development to become the "crowning achievement of suburban development" and he feared that nouveau riche Hollywood types would lower his property values.

In other respects, Bell was a farsighted developer. He carved roads out of hillsides and installed sewer, power, and water lines underground—expensive, but worth it. He also landscaped the place beautifully. The first tract he developed was two hundred acres, which he divided into parcels of several acres apiece, then encouraged buyers to purchase even larger lots of five and ten acres. He added polo fields, tennis courts, and my beloved Bel Air Country Club. He also built the Bel Air Stables on Stone Canyon Road and sixty-five miles of bridle paths.

And he installed the splendid gate at the Bel Air Road/Sunset Boulevard entrance. In the early days of the development, uniformed guards would patrol the entrance, making sure that no interlopers got in, and the private police force would escort visitors up the maze of streets to their destination.

All went swimmingly in the 1920s, but when the Depression hit, it was no time for artificial barriers to prospective buyers. Bel Air lots were going begging, and the area was teetering on insolvency, so Bell quietly let go of his strictures about movie people.

Colleen Moore, the popular flapper of the 1920s and a brilliant stock investor, bought a house on St. Pierre Road, and Warner Baxter came in about the same time. By World War II, movie people were setting up shop in Bel Air on a weekly basis, as it had become a more prestigious address than Beverly Hills. Judy Garland would build a ten-room Tudor house for herself at 1231 Stone Canyon Road, just up the street from the stables.

Bel Air had an interesting dynamic in those early years. Although you were only twenty minutes from Hollywood and its core industry, the town had a rural feel. Alphonzo Bell had his offices on Stone Canyon Road, and when he sold that property the office and the stables he had built there were redesigned and reconfigured to become the foundation of the Bel Air Hotel.

A lot of the rooms at the hotel were once horse stalls, and I'm particularly fond of a large circular fountain on one of the patios where I used to water my horse when I was a boy. Part of Bell's property was converted into the Bel Air Tea Room, where I bused tables as a kid, with John Derek working alongside me.

Besides busing the tables, I washed dishes and occasionally waited on tables. It sounds like a typical summer job, but it was a life changer, because I became close friends with another kid named Noel Clarebut. Noel introduced me to his mother, Helena, who ran the dining room and the antiques gallery at the hotel.

Helena became a tremendous influence on my life. A European, she loved the theater, food, classical music, dogs—all the finer things in life. I didn't have any of that. My family was Midwestern, with a utilitarian, bricks-and-mortar set of values.

Horses were very much a part of my life from the time we arrived. Robert Montgomery was responsible for making it easy to ride there, because he promoted the construction of bridle trails that wound their way through Bel Air in more scenic routes than were available in Beverly Hills.

My first horse was named Topper, after Hopalong Cassidy's horse. He was a great horse, and I had him until his old age, when my father did exactly as Robert Redford's character did in *The Electric Horseman*: he took Topper back to the breeder from whom he'd bought him. The breeder had a thousand acres, so Topper was unloaded into the pasture and slapped on the rear end, then went off to live out his days grazing. For Topper, life was a circle—he was born there, and he died there. At the time a lot of people didn't fuss over their animals; they were part of the property more than they were part of the family, but I'm proud to say that my father didn't feel that way, and he passed that same feeling on to me. Animals deserve nothing less.

Courtesy of the author

A photo of me with my horse Sonny.

Sonny was another horse I adored. He was a gentle soul, brown, with big hips and splashes of paint on his shoulders. Technically he was my father's horse, but Sonny and I bonded in a very special way. His previous owner had taught him a routine that I maintained and amplified at performances at shows and fairs.

We'd make an entrance with him pushing me out. I would pretend to trip and fall. Sonny would lie down next to me, and when he was flat on the ground I'd grab a strap that was around his stomach. He'd get up and lift me with him, and I would hop on his back. We'd make an exit, then come back with an American flag in Sonny's mouth. He'd toss his head a few times, which caused the flag to wave, and the crowd would reliably go nuts. Then he would take a bow.

For a boy who loved horses and was beginning to love applause, it was a surefire act, and a lot of fun to perform.

Years went by and Sonny got cataracts, so, just as he had with Topper, my dad took him back to the breeder. I got a chance to say good-bye to him, but losing him bothered me for years. It still does.

It sounds impossible now, almost like something out of science fiction, but the fact is that before and after World War II Los Angeles had one of the best mass transit systems in America. Electric streetcars connected Orange, Ventura, Riverside, and San Bernardino Counties with no exhaust and no smog—the trolley lines ran on overhead electric wires.

Los Angeles and the suburbs around it were expanding exponentially all during my childhood, but the air remained remarkably clean. I know: I rode those streetcars because that's how I went to the movies. Occasionally I would take my bike and head to Westwood to see a movie. But if the film I wanted to see was in Hollywood, it was too far for the bike ride, so I'd walk from our house to UCLA, and grab a bus to Beverly Hills, then catch the trolley. (Occasionally, my father would drive my mother, my sister, and me, and sometimes he'd even come in with us.)

The trolleys began in 1894 with horse-drawn cars. By 1895 there was an electric rail line connecting Los Angeles and Pasadena, and a year after that a line opened that connected Los Angeles with what would become Hollywood and Beverly Hills, all the way to Santa Monica.

During World War I you could go from downtown Los Angeles to as far away as San Bernardino, San Pedro, or San Fernando on the trolleys. There was a trip called the Old Mission that went from Los Angeles to Busch Gardens, all the way to Pasadena and San Gabriel Mission. The Mount Lowe trolley, which was actually a cable car on narrow-gauge track, went to the top of Echo Mountain.

Two trackless trolleys (the first in America) running through Laurel Canyon.

The Balloon Route ran from Los Angeles through Hollywood, Santa Monica, Venice Beach, Redondo, and back to Los Angeles via Culver City. (I shudder to think how long that round trip must have taken.)

Apparently the trolleys took a hit in the 1920s as the population became more prosperous and people started buying cars, but with World War II, gasoline and tire rationing revived the trolley lines, and ridership hit an all-time high of 109 million in 1944.

By then, Los Angeles had two separate trolley systems, commonly known as the Red Cars and the Yellow Cars. Pacific Electric owned the Red Car line, and National City Lines owned the Yellow Cars.

I generally took the Red Cars, which ran from Union Station downtown all the way to the beach—an east-west line. To get there, it wound through the middle of Beverly Hills, through the upper part of Hollywood, then crossed over to Sunset. The Red Cars were great—they were fifty feet long, and ran between forty and fifty miles an hour.

The transit system was remarkably well engineered, efficient, and, in modern terms, environmentally sound. When I was riding the Red and Yellow lines they were at their height—there were nine hundred Red Cars running on 1,150 miles of track covering four counties. There aren't that many people who remember them anymore, but they were a crucial factor in how Los Angeles developed the way it did. Because the trolleys made travel simple—not to mention cheap—they encouraged very expansive development. As late as 1930, more than 50 percent of the land in the LA basin was undeveloped. The population spread out over a very large area of land, which is why in my memory, and in my friends' memories, Los Angeles seemed uncrowded and undeveloped—almost sylvan.

Courtesy of the author

One of the red cars passing in front of Grauman's Chinese Theater on Hollywood Boulevard. In an astonishing coincidence, Grauman's just happens to be showing one of my movies.

Of course, it all changed. The sheer expanse of Southern California made it perfect for the automobile, and the basic disposition of the American public toward independence probably made the decline of the trolleys inevitable. Making the changeover faster than it had to be was the dismantling of streetcar systems in favor of buses by a number of companies, including General Motors, Firestone, and Standard Oil, who stood to make a lot more money with buses than with electric power.

By the early 1950s, when I was a young leading man at 20th Century Fox, cars had displaced the trolleys as the primary means of travel in Southern California. Freeways that sixty years later are now often impassable, not to mention impossible, were being constructed. By 1959 the only trolley line that was still operating was LA to Long Beach, and that was discontinued in 1961. The trolley cars were chopped up and destroyed; some were sunk off the coast. It was a terrible waste of valuable historical artifacts.

If you want to see remnants of the great Los Angeles trolley cars, you can go to a museum in Perris, California, seventy-four miles (by freeway!) from Los Angeles, where they have both Red Cars and Yellow Cars on display. Now the only way you can enjoy even a vestige of trolley culture is to go to downtown Los Angeles and ride Angel's Flight, a historical funicular that takes you just three hundred feet uphill.

One of the favored places in Southern California is the beach, where it's warmer in winter and cooler in summer than it is farther inland. When people wanted to get out of town completely in the warmer months, they would often head for Big Bear or Lake

Arrowhead, where the Arrowhead Springs Hotel was partially fi-nanced by Darryl Zanuck, Al Jolson, Joe Schenck, Claudette Col-bert, Constance Bennett, and a few others.

(A word about celebrity financiers—they were usually like ce-lebrities today who invest in sports teams. The amount of money that actually changed hands was minor; the stars were given some of the perks of ownership in return for whatever glamour their ce-lebrity brought to the establishment.)

The Arrowhead Springs Hotel was in San Bernardino, in the mountains about two hours away from Los Angeles. When it opened in December 1939, its advertising proclaimed it "the swank-iest spot in America," and it just might have been. The "springs" element was not just an advertising slogan—the hotel was in fact constructed over hot springs that ran to 202 degrees Fahrenheit.

The resort was primarily the vision of Jay Paley, the uncle of CBS's William Paley. The hotel was U-shaped, had 150 rooms spread over six floors, and three dining rooms. The most distin-guishing thing about Arrowhead Springs was its interior, which was designed by Dorothy Draper. She rarely ventured west of the Mississippi, and certainly never soiled her hands with any project that would be patronized by show business types.

Draper was the designer for the millions; she had a column in *Good Housekeeping* and wrote bestselling books. What she ended up doing at Arrowhead Springs was a top-to-bottom design of the sort that was rare for the era. She designed *everything*. The dining rooms were done in black and white; they had oversize black-lacquered Chinese cabinets on the walls, huge plaster light fixtures, pink and white roses on the tables. The doormen wore forest green with red trim and silver buttons; the cocktail lounge was done in bleached walnut and Delft tiles. The swizzle sticks were black and red.

I went there only once or twice, and I can tell you that it felt like money. It also felt predominantly feminine, as if you were trapped in a layout from *Vogue* magazine circa 1940. Had it been 1940, it might have been more tolerable, but I was there somewhere around 1954. The Arrowhead Springs Hotel was in operation until 1962.

As it turned out, more people were interested in being by the Pacific Ocean than they were in poaching themselves in hot springs.

Six Hollywood fashion models at the Arrowhead Springs Hotel, circa 1948.

They headed down to the ocean, first to Santa Monica, and then, as Santa Monica got crowded, to Malibu.

Malibu began to become more desirable, and gradually became more exclusive since there's less land there. Oddly, however, it took longer to settle than Santa Monica. In 1891, the Rindge family bought all thirteen thousand acres of what was then called Rancho Malibu for ten dollars an acre. The Rindges held on to the property for more than thirty years, finally letting go in 1927. It was only then that show people began settling in what came to be known as Malibu Colony.

In 1930 or so, you could lease a lot with thirty feet of ocean frontage for thirty dollars a month. Dozens of people took advantage of that bargain, including Barbara Stanwyck, Warner Baxter, John Gilbert, and three great friends: Ronald Colman, William Powell, and Richard Barthelmess.

The colony in those days was protected by a high stone wall, with a gate manned by an armed guard. When I got to California, they were starting to build houses to the south of the colony, and even in the mountains alongside the Pacific Coast Highway.

By then Malibu residents had also begun looking out to the ocean, to see what they could see. What they saw was . . . Catalina. Literally. But that wasn't unusual; all through the 1940s and into the 1950s you could see Catalina from Malibu. It seems impossible to believe now, but in that era you could even see Catalina from the hills above Hollywood, right up until the era when smog began to develop.

The particular charm of Catalina has always been that it's basically uninhabited. Twenty-two miles long and eight miles wide, the island is home to only about four thousand people, the vast majority of them living in Avalon, the town's only incorporated city.

Like Malibu, Catalina was for a long time the province of a single family—the Wrigleys, of chewing gum fame, who bought the island in 1919. William Wrigley Jr. spent the rest of his life preserving and promoting Catalina, and the fact that it remains so pristine is a testament to his foresight.

But Wrigley wasn't the first to see something special in Catalina. George Shatto, who was, like me, from Michigan (Grand Rapids, to be exact), had bought the island for two hundred thousand dollars in 1887. It was Shatto who founded Avalon, and it was his sister who gave that city its name, inspired by the idyllic island Avalon referenced in Tennyson's cycle of poems *Idylls of the King.*

But Shatto went bust, and the island existed in an uneasy limbo for a number of years. Los Angeles was only twenty miles away, and everybody knew that Catalina was destined to be some kind of vacation destination, but no one knew when its day would come.

World War I put a crimp in tourism. When it was over, Bill Wrigley, flush with money, was looking for something to be altruistic about, and Catalina turned out to be his project. Wrigley opened a mine there, along with a rock quarry, and he even started a plant that produced stunningly beautiful decorative tiles that he called Catalina Clay Products. All this only increased his passion for the island; he built a house on a hill overlooking the harbor and Avalon.

At that point, there were only two ships daily transporting people back and forth from the island to the mainland. Wrigley doubled the roster of ships, so now a lot more people could visit Catalina. In 1926, there were 622,000 visitors; four years later, the total was 700,000. What they saw was a very lightly managed natural wonderland, both on land and beneath the sea—Wrigley also kept a fleet of glass-bottom boats so that people could safely admire the marine life.

Most of the tourists were day-trippers, but they left a lot of money behind. I've been told that George S. Patton met his wife Beatrice on Catalina when they were children, but I'm not old enough to know if that's true.

The movies came to Catalina gradually. In 1920 Harry Houdini did some filming there for *Terror Island*. Buster Keaton's *The Navigator* was filmed off Avalon Bay. And whenever the studios needed a place to stand in for the South Pacific, they usually went to Catalina, as MGM did for the 1935 version of *Mutiny on the Bounty*.

By then Wrigley had built a splendid Art Deco dance hall called the Catalina Casino, which opened in 1929; the lower level houses a theater, the upper level the world's largest circular ballroom. The influx of population made the island a kind of artist's colony. Not only that, but the Chicago Cubs, which just happened to be owned by Wrigley, trained on the island from 1921 to 1951, with time out for World War II, when the island was used as a military training facility. From Wrigley's study, he could watch the Cubs work out their winter kinks during spring training.

In the days before and after the war, Catalina was all about yachting, although there was also a smattering of aviators. The boaters clustered at either the Hotel St. Catherine or the La Conga Club, which had a private dock reserved for members' boats. There were two yacht clubs: the Catalina Island Yacht Club in Avalon Bay, and the Isthmus Yacht Club in Two Harbors, whose building was built in 1864 as barracks for the Union Army. Then there was Moonstone Cove, a private cove operated by the Newport Harbor Yacht Club, and White's Landing, just west of Moonstone, with two yacht club camps. I had a mooring at Emerald Bay for years.

Catalina offered superb fishing; the waters were roiling with garibaldi, yellowtail, kelp, white sea bass, giant sea bass, and bonito. And there were great numbers of abalone, although now they've been fished out.

Beyond fish that made for great eating, there were also barracuda, bat rays, horn sharks, and the occasional great white shark, the latter of which usually appeared on the west—or ocean—side of the island. I also remember the awe-inspiring sight of large schools of flying fish sailing out of the water.

It was in the 1930s that Catalina became a getaway for Hollywood folks. It now seems that I must have spent half my adolescence and young manhood on Catalina, and the other half at the Bel Air Country Club. How lucky can you get? I began spending a great deal of time at Catalina right after the war. John Ford and his crew of reprobates all docked their yachts at Avalon. Ward Bond was always there, as was Ford's daughter Barbara and, for a time, her fiancé Robert Walker, who was unsuccessfully trying to get over his broken marriage to Jennifer Jones. Wherever you found John Ford and Ward Bond, you also found John Wayne, not to mention character actors like Paul Fix.

Ford's group began organizing a series of softball games, and I was an occasional participant. I was Mr. Eager, happy to play anywhere, just to play. Mainly, I was at first base. Duke Wayne and Ward Bond had been football players at USC, and they were both natural athletes who also knew how to play baseball. The surprising thing was how competitive the games were. It was only a pickup game of softball, but as far as Wayne and Bond were concerned, it could have been the World Series—they both played to win. Ford was always there, but he didn't actually take part much, which was odd, because he had been a champion athlete in high school.

Catalina also played a big part in my becoming an actor. It was while spending time on the island that I met Stanley Anderson. His stepdaughter had been hurt in an accident, and I enjoyed cheering her up by doing impressions of movie stars. I didn't know then that Stanley was one of the founders of the Beverly Hills Hotel and had great connections in the movie industry. His stepdaughter liked me, and so Stanley would invite me on his boat. And later, he put in a good word for me with various directors and casting directors.

Stanley sent me to Solly Baiano, the casting director at Warner Bros. I did all my impressions for Solly—Cagney, Bogart, etc.—and he responded by saying, "That's all very well, but we've already got Cagney and we've already got Bogart. What about doing *you?*"

I was totally stumped. "I can't do me," I said. "I don't know who me is."

It took a few years, but I eventually figured out who I was. By that time I wasn't under contract to Warner's, but to Fox.

Natalie and I spent a lot of time when we were courting on my first boat, a twenty-six-foot twin-screw Chris-Craft I had named *My Lady*. Natalie had never been to Catalina before I took her there, and it became one of her favorite places. After we got married the first time, we bought a thirty-two-foot Chris-Craft that we called *My Other Lady*.

In 1975 Phil Wrigley, the son of Bill Jr., deeded his family's shares in the island over to the Catalina Island Conservatory, which controls 88 percent of the island. The island's natural resources include six species of plants that are found only there. Other species unique to Catalina include the island fox, which was nearly wiped out by a strain of distemper; the population, which was down to less than one hundred animals in the 1990s, has now been restored to a level of over a thousand.

Then there are the buffalo. Yes, buffalo. How, you ask, did buffalo end up on this island? As with so much else, blame it on the
movies. In 1924 Paramount brought fourteen buffalo to the island
for a scene in their epic western *The Vanishing American*. When it
was through shooting the scenes, the company decided to just leave
the buffalo instead of going to the trouble of shipping them back to
the mainland.

If you've seen *The Vanishing American*, you're probably scratching
your head—there are no buffalo in the movie. That's because Paramount cut the scenes shot on Catalina. Ah, the wonders of the
movie business!

But those fourteen buffalo flourished. The herd has grown over
the years to about 150, and their numbers remain at that self-
sustaining level. What the Wrigley family did for Catalina meant
that the island remains one of the few unspoiled places in Southern
California . . . and indeed the world.

As the movie industry expanded, the population needed more vacation destinations, which inexorably led to Palm Springs. The
Springs got going in 1934, when Charlie Farrell and Ralph Bellamy
bought up fifty-two acres of desert for thirty-five hundred dollars
and started the Racquet Club as a way to defray some of their costs.
Much to their surprise, it became a popular gathering spot for Hollywood actors who wanted to get out of town for a long weekend.
Before the Racquet Club, there had been only the Desert Inn, which
had been there since 1909 and was patronized mostly by victims of
tuberculosis, who took bubbling mud baths at twenty-five cents a
dip under the supervision of local Indians. A few years after the
Racquet Club came the Palm Springs Tennis Club, but for the

Everett Collection

Here I am doing the publicity thing at Palm Springs Racquet Club.

movie people the Racquet Club was always the main destination. Soon, the Racquet Club and all of Palm Springs had become a very posh resort. At that point, the main activities were tennis and horse-back riding.

The attraction of Palm Springs was its hot, dry climate and complete seclusion, far from the studios and the gossip columnists. For years Palm Springs was one of the places you went if you were playing around on your spouse, or wanted to. The combination of a resort culture with geographical remoteness made for some wild times. As far as the people, it was the crème de la crème of the industry.

What was wonderful about Palm Springs was that it was an

Playing in a singles match at Palm Springs Racquet Club.

entirely different environment than Los Angeles, and yet it was only two hours away. Palm Springs is surrounded by mountains—the San Bernardino Mountains to the north, the Santa Rosa Mountains to the south, the San Jacinto Mountains to the west, and the Little San Bernardino Mountains to the east. It's situated in a valley, and gets unbelievably hot in the summer—a temperature of 106 is normal, and it can go even higher, then falling to anywhere from 77 to 90 degrees at night.

But that's in the summer. In the winter, it's idyllic; it rarely gets over 85 degrees or so, and the nights are cool.

The first time I went to Palm Springs was before World War II with my father. I was immediately enchanted. We went riding in the desert, and tied our horses up at a place in Cathedral City where we bought delicious fresh orange juice.

Palm Springs then was the sort of town with no streetlights—after dark, the only illumination was the moon, but in the desert that's much brighter than you think. I remember the mountains, the orange groves, the swimming pools, the desert sunsets, the air—so invigorating I always believed the oxygen content had to be higher than in the city.

Even then, the town had great bars. Don the Beachcomber's had a beachhead there, as did the Doll House. And there was a restaurant called Ruby Dunes, which became one of Frank Sinatra's favorite places.

Eventually, the unique environment of Palm Springs called for unique kinds of houses, and American modernist architects like Richard Neutra flourished there. Neutra's Kaufmann House—built for the same man who'd commissioned Frank Lloyd Wright's Fallingwater in Pennsylvania—was built in 1946.

Neutra stole at least one of my friend the great California architect Cliff May's central ideas: the place is built around a courtyard and includes a fair amount of natural materials—the stone walls and chimney came from nearby quarries and match up with the colors of the adjacent San Jacinto Mountains. And Neutra went with an early version of xeriscaping, as he filled the front yard with large boulders and desert plants that didn't need much water.

Neutra's success in Palm Springs brought more commissions, and more modernist architects followed in his wake, although few of them had Neutra's dominating personality. "I am not International Style," he once said. "I am Neutra!" It wasn't long before John Lautner, Albert Frey, and Rudolph Schindler were building there as well. The result was that Palm Springs became a hotbed of modified Bauhaus aesthetics. But when I was first going there, most of the architecture was Mexican or Spanish villas.

In the '60s, the houses were open in design, with air-conditioning—Palm Springs could never have been settled in a large way without the invention of air-conditioning—and windows that made the desert landscape part of the dwelling.

I remember the Palm Springs of my youth as something out of a western movie or, more specifically, a dude ranch. It was very western; hotel employees dressed up as if they were the Sons of the Pioneers, in embroidered shirts and cowboy boots. The bartender at the Racquet Club was actually named Tex. Tex, the lawyer Greg Bautzer, and I once got into a big fight at the Racquet Club with a couple of obnoxious out-of-town drunks. Tex could not only mix a killer martini, he could also clean out a room, and quickly.

The important thing to note about Palm Springs is that it was actually a small town, an intimate place whose population was mostly an extension of Hollywood.

There was, for instance, Alan Ladd Hardware, which I suspect had been started by Ladd or his wife Sue Carol as a hedge against the vagaries of the movie business. It was actually a spectacularly well-stocked and successful store, and it was there for a long, long time. And I still remember Desmond's department store.

Among the other celebrities who lived in Palm Springs were Zane Grey, Sam Goldwyn, the composer Frederick Loewe, Dinah Shore, and Frank Sinatra. William Powell and his much younger wife Diana Lewis—everybody called her "Mousie"—had moved there after he retired, and I got to know him well.

As you might expect, Bill Powell was a gentleman. He was a good drinking man, and surprisingly self-effacing. One time I

Everett Collection

Yours truly having a good time at a party in Palm Springs, circa 1955.

complimented him on the marvelous series of movies he had made with Myrna Loy and the qualities he had brought to all of his films, but he didn't seem to think they, or he, were all that much.

"I never really did anything different," he said, referring to his career. I thought he was being unfair to himself, and still do.

In the 1950s, Palm Springs began to change. When I first went there with my father, it had precisely one golf course: the O'Donnell, a little nine-holer. But soon other courses sprang up—Thunderbird, Tamarisk—and later the Eisenhower Medical Center changed the nature of the town. It became far more of a retirement community than it ever had been, and the geriatric influence shifted the nature of the town—it became less exuberant, more sedate. At the same time, it also became less seasonal and more of a year-round place.

Frank Sinatra started out by buying a little three-bedroom tract house near the Tamarisk Country Club and began remodeling and adding on until he had a very large compound with guesthouses, a helicopter pad, and a caboose that held his huge model train layout—Frank loved his Lionel trains. Next door to his own compound, he built a house for his mother, Dolly. Down the street Walter Annenberg had a private golf course.

For years, we would go to Frank's for New Year's Eve. Dean Martin would be there, as would Sammy Davis Jr., perhaps Angie Dickinson. Frank appreciated the remoteness of Palm Springs but also liked the fact that the place wasn't so remote he'd be deprived of the amenities he wanted. By the time he was finished with the house, it had a walk-in freezer and a huge dining room that sat twenty-four people. The interior decoration made some of the place look like a luxurious modern hotel, but I always figured that was because Frank had spent so much of his life in hotels that it was the kind of environment in which he felt comfortable.

Eventually I moved to Palm Springs, too, when I married my second wife, Marion, in the early 1960s, and my kids went to school there. We lived there for seven years—seven very happy years. My house was built out of desert rock and was Spanish in design—Herman Wouk lives there now. That house was just a bit away from the house that had been built by Zane Grey, and it was right across the street from one of King Gillette's houses.

My proximity to Zane Grey's house was thrilling to me. I'd read his novels as a boy, and knew he'd been a great outdoorsman who had done a great deal to popularize deep-sea fishing. It always

My future wife, Jill, and Frank at the very first Frank Sinatra
Golf Tournament in Palm Springs, circa 1960.

delighted me to think how we could have been neighbors if Grey
hadn't gone and died.

When Natalie and I married for the second time, in 1972, I still
had the house, and we decided to settle there. We added some
rooms on, and when our daughter, Courtney, was born, we raised
her there. Then we bought our house in Beverly Hills from Patti
Page.

There were other places where people went to get away, some of
them pretty far afield. Gamblers often went over the border to Tijuana, Agua Caliente, and Ensenada. It's an open question who was
the biggest gambler in Hollywood, the answer known only to ac-
countants of the period. I'd put my money on either David O.

Selznick or Joe Schenck, the latter of whom actually had a casino in his house, although when the police closed it down Joe claimed he didn't know about it.

Uh-huh.

Then there was Harry Cohn, founder of Columbia Pictures. Cohn's annual one-month vacation took place at Saratoga Race Course, and he is said to have averaged five thousand to ten thousand dollars a day in bets. This went on until he hit a cold streak and lost four hundred thousand dollars.

A normal man might have had a nervous breakdown over losing that amount of money—I know I would. In fact, Cohn's brother, a cofounder of the studio, had to warn him that he would be removed from the presidency of Columbia Pictures if he didn't get his gambling under control.

So Harry Cohn slowly put aside horses in favor of betting on football, and cut back to betting only about fifty dollars on college games.

It makes perfect sense that many of the moguls were, in fact, serious gamblers, because spending millions of dollars on a movie is nothing if not a gamble. B. P. Schulberg, who ran Paramount in the early 1930s, was a particularly degenerate gambler, and it ruined his career. There were quiet poker games around town as well, and people like Eddie Mannix, Joe Schenck, Sid Grauman, Norman Krasna, and the Selznick brothers were regular participants. A lot of money changed hands on these outings; the story goes that B. P. Schulberg once dropped a hundred thousand dollars in one night— and this at a time when a hundred thousand dollars was serious money, even in Hollywood. The Selznicks came by their habit naturally; their father had ruined his business by gambling.

Interestingly, almost all of the town's serious bettors were men;

of the women, only Constance Bennett is said to have been able to hold her own at the poker tables. Clifton Webb told me that whoever was hosting the game would bank the money the next morning—nobody wanted to walk around with hundreds of thousands of dollars—and checks would be handed out later that day.

I was close friends with Connie Bennett's husband Gilbert Roland, with whom I worked in *Beneath the 12-Mile Reef.* It seems that one night Gil lost fifty thousand dollars at the poker game. The problem was that Gil didn't have fifty thousand dollars, or anything even close to it, so Connie had to make the debt good. As she handed over the check, she said, "Oh, the fucking I'm getting for the fucking I'm getting."

Gil was a spectacular-looking man, very passionate, extremely romantic. He would talk about his remarkable history with women, but not in a graphic way. Women meant a great deal to him; life meant a great deal to him.

Gambling has always been one of the main participatory sports in Hollywood, always illegal, often tolerated, usually thriving. In *The Big Sleep* Raymond Chandler wrote about a place called the Cypress Club, a barely disguised version of the Clover Club, which was above the Sunset Strip, just west of the Chateau Marmont.

Opened in 1933, the Clover Club was the creation of Billy Wilkerson, director Raoul Walsh, and Al and Lew Wertheimer. The only way to gain entrance to the Clover Club was through membership—i.e., money—or if they knew you.

The food was excellent at the Clover Club, but the main attraction was gambling. The Clover Club, along with other, less renowned venues, were variations on the speakeasies that had thrived during Prohibition.

It was surprising how well known these places were, even

though they were ostensibly illegal. Radio broadcasts featured them. The newspapers covered them as well, noting that such people as David Selznick and Gregory Ratoff—also a heavy gambler—were patronizing the Clover Club. Some clubs even advertised, usually using the word "exclusive" in the copy. When the Clover closed, Lew Wertheimer went on the payroll at Fox because Joe Schenck was into him for serious money. The Fox stockholders helped him pay it off.

Then there were the gambling ships moored just beyond the three-mile limit. One of them was the *Tango*, which began operating off Venice Beach in 1929 and was still there ten years later. The *Johanna Smith* billed itself as "the world's most famous gambling ship." But the one that seemed the most heavily patronized was the *Rex*, which was moored off Santa Monica for years, in full view of shore. To ferry people out to the *Rex*, there were three barges and a fleet of water taxis. The ads in the newspapers announced:

Only 10 minutes from Hollywood, plus a comfortable
10-minute boat ride to the REX.
25 cents round trip from Santa Monica pier at foot
of Colorado Street, Santa Monica.
Ship opens at 12:30 p.m. daily.

From the way the ships were presented, you would have thought you were boarding the *Queen Mary*. Actually, the *Rex* was a converted fishing barge that looked . . . like a converted fishing barge, even though an ex-con named Tony Cornero had spent a quarter million dollars to convert it. But its unlovely appearance was much less important than what happened on board.

The ship itself had a 250-foot glass-covered gaming deck

The notorious gambling ship *The Rex.*

offering faro, roulette, and craps. Everybody's gambling tastes could
be accommodated, from high rollers to the penny ante. There were
three hundred slot machines, a bingo parlor that seated five hundred people, six roulette tables, eight dice tables, keno. . . . There
was even a complicated setup for offtrack betting. On a lower deck
there was dancing and entertainment, a café, and several bars.

The *Rex* could accommodate two thousand customers, and its
daily profit could be as much as ten thousand dollars. To keep their
profits safe from bandits, the boat was heavily fortified by security
with a generous supply of machine guns.

Soon the waters off the California coast were dotted by gambling ships hovering outside the three-mile limit: the *Monte Carlo,*
the *City of Panama*, the *Texas*, the *Showboat*, the *Caliente*. One ship,
the *Playa*, wasn't satisfied with the three-mile limit, and sailed
twelve miles out, which was not only beyond Los Angeles County
jurisdiction but beyond federal jurisdiction. The *Playa* served
out-of-season food that was forbidden on land—elaborate stuff, but
great stuff. In order to get people onto those boats, they hustled
everybody and everything.

Supposedly law enforcement personnel were very frustrated by
the presence of the *Rex* and the rest of the ships, but I don't believe
it. None of the many underground enticements of Los Angeles

before and after World War II would have been possible without the apathy of or, more likely, the acquiescence of the police. The amount of payoffs from the gambling houses of Los Angeles and Hollywood that padded the pockets of the cops must have been nearly equivalent to their profits. It was an environment that spawned a lot of James Ellroy novels.

The gambling ships came to an end just before World War II, when California attorney general Earl Warren got serious and went after them, using as a wedge the fact that the water taxis that ferried the customers back and forth weren't registered as public vehicles.

Only a few years later Las Vegas was born out of an effort to service the gamblers of Los Angeles.

But before Vegas there was Agua Caliente, a resort just across the Mexican border built for the specific purpose of enabling Americans to indulge in the pleasurable activity that was forbidden in their native country: gambling.

Agua Caliente was the brainchild of Baron Long, a man who ran gambling and bootlegging outfits around Los Angeles, usually skirting the law by operating just outside the city limits in unincorporated towns like Vernon or beyond the three-mile limit at sea.

In 1926 Long decided to take advantage of the "anything goes" atmosphere of Mexico and build a spa at Agua Caliente Hot Springs, six miles from Tijuana. There was no shortage of investors; I believe some of the original generation of movie moguls, such as Joe Schenck, came in on the deal. Joe supposedly spent something close to half a million dollars building the resort and casino.

Joe Schenck was such an interesting man. He and his brother Nick controlled three movie studios: Nick ran Loew's Incorporated, the parent company of MGM, while Joe, after a very successful career as an independent producer, first ran United Artists, then left to form 20th Century pictures with Darryl Zanuck, which soon took over the moribund Fox organization and became 20th Century Fox—the studio that signed me in 1949.

The resort's grounds didn't look like much originally—just scrub with sycamore trees—but by the time it opened in June 1928, after millions of dollars in construction costs, the landscape had been radically altered. Occupying 655 acres, it even had its own airport, with easier access for those long weekends. It was an immediate success, because it was the only game out of town. If you wanted the types of things Agua Caliente offered, you had to go to Agua Caliente.

The centerpiece of the resort was a four-hundred-room luxury hotel. Well, that's not really true—the centerpiece was the casino, where roulette, baccarat, and faro were played. And after the casino came the racetrack. The racetrack attracted people who wouldn't be caught dead in a casino—Gary Cooper was there, as were Bing Crosby and Clark Gable, Jean Harlow and Howard Hughes.

Occasionally, a film would shoot there—the location was visually interesting, and there were plenty of ways to pass the time at night. When Jackie Cooper goes hunting for his alcoholic father around a luxury hotel in *The Champ*, he's searching Agua Caliente. There was even a Warner Bros. movie called *In Caliente*, featuring the great Busby Berkeley number "The Lady in Red."

While the hotel's exterior looked like something left over from the mission days, inside it was another story entirely. There was an Art Deco dining room inspired by the 1925 Paris exhibition, plus a Moorish-style spa and a Louis XIV–inspired room.

It was the height of a certain kind of luxury. Even the barbershop, which had only three chairs, flaunted custom-designed terra-cotta. The power plant had a 150-foot-high smokestack that was tiled and covered with decorative ironwork so that it resembled an Istanbul minaret.

So much of what would make Vegas Vegas was actually devised at Agua Caliente. Food, for instance, was a loss leader—they charged only a dollar for a sumptuous lunch, and the casino was without clocks or windows. Sound familiar?

Agua Caliente did not set out to compete with Palm Springs or Catalina; it was designed to attract the same clientele as the Riviera or Palm Beach. And for a time, it succeeded. Movie people loved it. Aside from Joe Schenck, other shareholders included Al Jolson, Irving Berlin, and Alexander Pantages. In 1933, Schenck purchased control of the resort and positioned himself on the board of directors, along with Douglas Fairbanks Sr. and Jesse Lasky.

And then it all came crashing down. In 1935 the president of Mexico signed an executive order outlawing gambling. Two days later, the resort shut down.

Conveniently, just a few years earlier, Nevada had passed legislation allowing gambling, which meant that it was just a question of time until everything that made Caliente Caliente would be available without having to cross the border. Mexico eventually nationalized the old resort and used it as an education facility, although three fires in the 1960s and a misguided urban renewal program in 1975 wiped out the facility as a whole. But for a few years, Caliente was the site of a gaudy spree that eventually landed close to home.

The Houses and Hotels

Billy Wilder could do a lot of things, and setting a scene was one of them.

"I had landed myself in the driveway of some big mansion that looked run-down and deserted," says William Holden as Joe Gillis at the opening of *Sunset Boulevard*. "It was a great big white elephant of a place. The kind crazy movie people built in the crazy twenties."

Billy's attitude was typical. The rap against the architecture of Los Angeles was that it was nothing but a conglomeration of warring styles. But that's because Los Angeles had a very small indigenous population; it was settled by people who streamed there before and after World War I. All these new arrivals were from different parts of the world and all of them had different ideas of taste; with the exception of the Mission style that was the legacy of Spanish California, there was no strong architectural tradition to guide a building boom.

Initially the movie people settled in and around Hollywood Boulevard, and the bungalows that had been part of the initial settlement around 1900 were replaced by the Spanish Mediterranean look that became the first wave of popular style.

There were also apartments that catered to the movie people who were holding on to their money to see whether this movie thing had any permanence. A lot of them were built around courtyards, with fountains and Spanish tile. Of these, the most elaborate was the Garden Court, which stood on Hollywood Boulevard into the 1970s. Sixty years earlier the Garden Court had refused to take people from the movie industry, with very few exceptions, such as the very proper Englishman J. Stuart Blackton, who founded the early motion picture firm Vitagraph.

But if blame is to be apportioned for what Beverly Hills is today, it should probably go to Douglas Fairbanks.

In the beginning, Beverly Hills was all beans, acres of beans, and the only people who lived there were Mexican migrant workers. But after 1900, oil was discovered in what would become West Hollywood and land began changing hands. The land was now too valuable to be relegated to farmland, so it was divided up into residential lots.

To do the landscaping and planning, the landscape architect Wilbur Cook Jr. was hired. Cook had worked on the design of the 1893 World's Columbian Exposition in Chicago alongside Frederick Law Olmsted, who was famed for his design of New York's Central Park.

Cook laid out a three-tier system. People without a lot of money were relegated to small lots in the area around Wilshire and Santa Monica Boulevards. The area of Beverly Hills that lay "below the tracks" of the Pacific Electric railroad along Santa Monica Boulevard came with restrictive covenants that forbade blacks or Asians from buying, owning, or even residing there except as live-in servants. Cook also made space for a commercial zone that was close to the large houses and estates to the north.

North of Santa Monica and south of Sunset was for the upper middle class, with large houses, wide lots, and streets lined with trees of identical size and species. (These guys left nothing to chance.) The hills above Sunset Boulevard were reserved for mansions.

What Cook wanted to avoid was a grid plan of straight lines and squares, which would inevitably lead to views of empty fields extending toward the ocean. What he designed were largely curving streets, which led to a procession of constantly changing views. He used garden hoses to mark off the curves of the streets, forming the borders of the roads. The curves created a feeling of coziness, of community.

The first lots went on sale for eight hundred to a thousand dollars an acre, with a 10 percent discount if paid in cash and another 10 percent discount if construction started within a year. The original streets were Rodeo, Beverly, Canon, and Crescent Drives. Beverly Park sat between Beverly and Canon, which had a beautiful koi pond and a sign announcing that you were now in Beverly Hills—as if there could be any doubt.

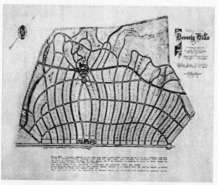

Wilbur Cook's original plan for Beverly Hills.
Notice the winding, curvy roads.

For a long time, Beverly Hills remained quite barren because most of the movie people were still living around Hollywood proper, or in Crescent Heights or Los Feliz. Seeing that lots weren't moving, a developer named Burton Green figured that a hotel might stimulate a land rush. (For many years, it was believed that Green had named the town after Beverly Farms, his home in Massachusetts, but that's not true. Green's own version of the naming of Beverly Hills is as follows: "I happened to read a newspaper article which mentioned that President [William Howard] Taft was vacationing in Beverly, Massachusetts . . . It struck me that Beverly was a pretty name. I suggested the name 'Beverly Hills' to my associates; they liked it, and the name was accepted." Given the natural beauty of the location, they could have called it Hogwarts and it probably would have been successful.)

In early February 1911, Green hired Margaret Anderson and her son to open and operate a luxury hotel.

Margaret had originally come to California in the 1870s. She'd married, had two children, and worked in the orange business. After a nasty divorce, she took over a boardinghouse in Westlake, and in 1902 the Hollywood Hotel. So Margaret and her son Stanley were Hollywood pioneers, the hospitality equivalent of Cecil B. DeMille.

Margaret's motto was "Our guests are entitled to the best of everything, regardless of cost." In the early days the Hollywood Hotel had forty rooms. The hotel cost—wait for it!—the munificent sum of twenty-five thousand dollars, and was designed by Oliver Perry Dennis and Lyman Farwell, who also designed the building that would become the Magic Castle in Hollywood. The Magic Castle is still standing; I wish I could say the same for the Hollywood Hotel.

Two people could stay at the hotel for $32.50 a week. For that

Construction of the Hollywood Hotel, circa 1905.

money, you also got a private bath and all your meals—a bargain. While his mother ran the hotel, Stanley took on a leadership role in the community at large—first in Hollywood, later in Beverly Hills. Stanley knew everybody, was friends with everybody: industrialists, entrepreneurs, and, of course, celebrities. He also began dabbling in real estate, buying property on Rodeo Drive. Stanley's son once expounded to me about his father's wisdom in buying retail corner lots. Unfortunately, I never took the advice to heart.

When Burton Green had the idea for the Beverly Hills Hotel, the obvious choice to run it was Margaret Anderson and her son.

Photos taken during construction in 1911 show nothing much there other than a huge, flat, open field and a water wagon for the workers.

The hotel itself was built to resemble a Franciscan mission, with a white stucco exterior and terra-cotta Spanish tile roof. The original promotional brochure laid it all out in the soothing tones beloved of advertising travel writers since the beginning of time: "Every time one thinks of California he thinks of sunny romance and gold; of sunny skies and balmy breezes; of whispering palms and sandy beaches and gently booming surf. He thinks of climate the like of which is not equaled in any other part of the world. . . .

Here in Southern California's most entrancing spot on the main road halfway between Los Angeles and the Sea is the Beverly Hills Hotel."

On the day it opened in 1912, Green's investment totaled half a million dollars—a huge sum in 1912. It was generally felt that the hotel was so far off the beaten track that it was sure to fail, but it quickly became quite popular, helped along by a Pacific Electric trolley line that stopped directly in front of the entrance. Thus, travelers could get off the train in Los Angeles and travel to the hotel with a minimum of fuss. But home sales still lagged in the area, and for a good ten years after it was constructed, the Beverly Hills Hotel continued to look out on nothing but empty fields.

The hotel soon became famous for its gardens, which certainly figured to attract Midwesterners from the frigid plains of Iowa and Kansas. Stanley devised a brilliant publicity strategy: the patrons of the hotel were encouraged to pick any of the flowers that grew in the gardens. Arranged in bouquets in the rooms, the flowers added a personal touch that made the guests feel right at home.

The hotel began building bungalows in 1915, which indicates that they were getting patronage from people who wanted to stay for the entire winter and for whom a hotel room would be too confining. The first five bungalows were in the Mission Revival style and had several bedrooms apiece—bring the entire family!—and a porch overlooking the main court of the hotel. By the 1930s, there would be more than twenty bungalows, scattered over the sixteen acres of gardens.

In 1915 among the amenities on offer were horseback rides before breakfast with a stable of Kentucky horses on the grounds. Then there was golf at the adjacent Los Angeles Country Club.

And believe it or not, there were fox hunts in the hills above the hotel, which tells you a lot about the guests who stayed there.

In 1919 Douglas Fairbanks, the first great swashbuckling star of the movies and as charismatic a man as ever walked in front of a camera, bought a glorified hunting lodge on Summit Drive, off Benedict Canyon, about a half mile above the Beverly Hills Hotel. He paid thirty-five thousand dollars for the place, and it wasn't much—it had six rooms, no electricity, no running water, and looked a little run-down.

And then it got worse. As Stanley Anderson's son told me the story a quarter century later, the morning after Fairbanks moved in, Stanley's phone rang. It was Fairbanks, and he was distraught. "I've never felt so awful," he said. "I have to leave Beverly Hills." It seemed that three of his new neighbors had called him the night before and told him that actors weren't welcome in the town. Property values, and so forth.

Stanley happened to know the neighbors in question—Stanley knew everybody. First he managed to calm Fairbanks down; then he defused the situation by calming the neighbors down. Fairbanks decided to stay and began remodeling and greatly enlarging the old lodge. Soon afterward he married Mary Pickford. It was a royal wedding, for Pickford was Fairbanks's opposite number: the King of Hollywood was marrying its queen.

Like almost all the early stars, Pickford was born poor. Her father had died young, and the only way the Toronto family could survive was for Mary—whose real name was Gladys Smith—to go onstage. She was very blond and very beautiful, and she became quite successful as a child actress, eventually going to work for the famous theatrical producer David Belasco. That led to work with

D. W. Griffith at the Biograph studio on the Lower East Side of
New York, which in turn led to a twenty-year career of success in
the movies.

Pickford and Fairbanks owned their own studios, owned their
own films, and, along with Charlie Chaplin and D. W. Griffith,
founded United Artists. They were all early examples of the actor
as entrepreneur, and they set a pattern that the most ambitious stars
replicate even today.

Chaplin and Fairbanks were best friends, and it was because of
Fairbanks that Charlie Chaplin also built a house on Summit Drive
in Beverly Hills in 1921. It certainly wasn't because he was in love
with the surrounding environment: "The alkali and the sagebrush
gave off an odorous, sour tang that made the throat dry and the
nostrils smart," wrote Chaplin in his memoirs. "In those days, Beverly Hills looked like an abandoned real estate development. Sidewalks ran along and disappeared into open fields and lampposts
with white globes adorning empty streets; most of the globes were
missing, shot off by passing revelers from roadhouses."

At night, Chaplin could hear the coyotes howling. Here was a
poor boy from London who shuddered at the very thought of coyotes, but to Fairbanks it was all impossibly romantic. So Chaplin
stayed.

After they married, Fairbanks and Pickford added another
wing to the house and a second floor, and they ripped out most of
the interior walls. Fairbanks's plans were as grand as his movies,
and he grew restless because the process was taking so long. So he
moved in lights from his movie studio and hired enough workers
for three eight-hour shifts. Fairbanks also landscaped the property
beautifully, with hundreds of trees and shrubs, and added a

swimming pool complete with a miniature sandy beach. Below the house was a stable that held six horses.

Christening their new home Pickfair, the couple moved in, and the world began beating a path to Beverly Hills. The house was decorated in a sedate style—the carpeting in Pickford's bedroom was a pale green, as were the silk curtains, while the dining room had a beamed ceiling, watered silk wallpaper, and a sideboard that held a good silver tea service.

The hall next to the living room had a beautiful terra-cotta tile floor for dancing, and the pale green of the bedroom was replicated in the living room, which had accents of yellow drapes, a couple of antique vases converted into lamps, and a nice Oriental rug over the hardwood floor.

A lot of the furniture—all dark wood and heavily carved—came from Los Angeles department stores. Eventually, the house was redecorated in a more eighteenth-century French tradition, although Fairbanks's enthusiasms virtually define the word "eclectic." He spent a good deal of money on Frederic Remington paintings. Once he paid five thousand dollars—a fortune at the time—for a prize German shepherd, and was probably the first American movie star to develop a passion for English tailoring, about which more later.

Unfortunately, parties at Pickfair could be a trifle sedate—Fairbanks didn't drink, and didn't want anyone else to drink, either, perhaps because his own father had been a drunk, perhaps because he was worried about the long history of alcoholism in his wife's family, which eventually afflicted Mary—the great tragedy of both their lives.

In those early years Fairbanks was quite the scamp. Frank Case, who ran the Algonquin Hotel in New York and knew a thing or two about the hospitality business, was a good friend of Fairbanks's, and told some stories that demonstrated both the star's boyish exuberance and how empty Beverly Hills was at the time.

According to Case, Fairbanks would climb into his Stutz Bearcat, shift into neutral, coast all the way down Summit Drive, and make it to the studio on Sunset and Vine without ever having to actually start his car. Occasionally, if he got bored, he'd skip the roads and cut across empty fields. Once, Fairbanks suggested that he might run alongside the car instead of sitting in it, just to keep things interesting.

These two people, both born into the lower middle class, became the hosts for kings and queens of Europe—Lord and Lady

Douglas Fairbanks and Mary Pickford in their swimming pool at Pickfair.

Mountbatten honeymooned at Pickfair, and every year a procession of dukes and duchesses descended to visit their dear friends Douglas and Mary. At other times they hosted Albert Einstein, F. Scott Fitzgerald, Babe Ruth, and H. G. Wells.

By greeting royalty as equals, they became royalty themselves, and some of that trickled down to the rest of Hollywood.

If I've spent a lot of time on Pickfair, it's a measure not only of the eminence of its owners, but of the formal yet approachable country gentleman style of the house, which became a sort of model for Beverly Hills, and for many of the developments that followed down through the years. Fairbanks and Pickford themselves set the example for world-class movie stars as they lived their lives with a stately dignity.

Chaplin lived at 1085 Summit Drive for the next thirty years, until he left America for Switzerland. Mary Pickford remained at Pickfair until her death in 1979. Douglas Fairbanks died in 1939, so I never met him, which I regret—he was a golf fanatic, so we would have had plenty to talk about.

After Doug and Mary, other stars followed. The area was now officially open for movie business, and the lawns and gardens of the Beverly Hills Hotel were frequently used for locations. Harold Lloyd, who would become a close friend and mentor of mine, would shoot scenes from his film *A Sailor-Made Man* there in 1921, and Charlie Chaplin would make *The Idle Class* right across the street, in Sunset Park.

The movie studios themselves soon followed. In 1925 William Fox bought 108 acres on the western border of Beverly Hills. His studio had been located at Sunset and Western in Hollywood since 1915, but Fox was an expansion-minded man and needed more space. Three years later he christened Fox Movietone Studios.

King Gillette, the founder of the shaving company, sold his first Hollywood house to Gloria Swanson, then commissioned a beautiful Spanish Colonial Revival house in Malibu Canyon from Wallace Neff.

The Gillette/Swanson house was at 904 North Crescent Drive, just north of Sunset and across the street from the main entrance to the Beverly Hills Hotel. It was a modest little cottage—115 feet wide and 100 feet deep, with twenty rooms spread over four acres. There were five bathrooms and an electric elevator to take you to the second floor. There was also a thousand-square-foot terrace that overlooked the lawns and a sweeping garden of acacias and palm trees.

The walls were hung with tapestries and draped in peacock silks. The mistress's bathroom was done in black marble with a golden tub. There was a movie theater and a large garden. When she entertained, butlers were dressed in full livery. Swanson was all of twenty years old when she bought the place from Gillette in 1919, and she was evidently seeking to replicate the swanky society dramas she was making for Cecil B. DeMille.

It was a dream palace, different from Pickfair, but equivalent in terms of its impact.

After Fairbanks and Chaplin built on the street, Tom Mix started construction on his own six-acre estate, at 1018 Summit Drive. It had a wall around the property by the side of the road, so you couldn't see too much of it, but you could always tell it was Tom Mix's house—there was a large neon sign mounted on the roof that flashed the letters "TM" to the night sky.

The Gold Rush was on.

Beverly Hills construction skyrocketed 1,000 percent within five years. Will Rogers was named honorary mayor of the town, and in his inauguration speech he announced the prevailing ethic, which would define show business: "I am for the common people, and as Beverly Hills has no common people, I'll be sure to make good." He then promised to give the city's nonexistent poor bigger swimming pools and wider bridle paths.

A house that was almost equal in fame to Pickfair belonged to Rudolph Valentino. Falcon Lair was located off Benedict Canyon Drive, past Summit Drive, at 1436 Bella Drive (now Cielo Drive). Falcon Lair was aptly named, because it was situated on eight acres on a promontory below which you could see the sparse (at the time) lights of the city below. Valentino paid $175,000 for the house and property in 1925, and was so compulsive about spending that he had only enough money for the down payment. He asked Joe Schenck, to whom he was under contract, for help in buying the place, because its owner didn't want to accept the actor's personal note—for good reasons, as it turned out. Joe was an obliging man, so he co-signed the loan. Valentino would live in it for a little more than a year before his sudden early death. But in that year he spent a huge amount of money he didn't have, redecorating the main house, putting up a nine-foot taupe wall around the property, building stables and kennels, and adding servants' quarters over the garage.

Falcon Lair was Spanish in style, with a red tile roof and stucco walls that were also painted taupe. The house was decorated rather like a set from one of Valentino's own larger-than-life romantic movies. The doors were imported from Florence, and there was a life-size portrait of the owner dressed in the costume of a Saracen warlord from the Crusades. The floor in the entry hall was travertine. The drapes were all of Genovese velvet, and the curtains in the master bedrooms were hand-loomed Italian net.

The house was primarily decorated with antiques—Turkish Arabian, Spanish screens, Florentine chairs, a French walnut chest from the fifteenth century. Valentino had thousands of books, and there were weapons and armor scattered throughout the house.

If all you saw were the main rooms, you might think the place looked like a museum of medieval artifacts. But in his bedroom Valentino indulged himself with an exotic range of colors. The king-size bed had gold ball feet, while the headboard was lacquered a dark blue. The sheets, pillowcases, and bedspread were crocus

Bettmann/CORBIS

A rear view of Rudolph Valentino's Hollywood home, Falcon Lair, which was built into the side of a high hill. Notice the aviary at bottom left.

yellow, as were his Japanese silk pajamas. There was an orange lacquer pedestal table at the foot of the bed that had a perfume lamp on it—when the lamp was turned on, the room would fill with fragrance.

The interesting thing about Falcon Lair was that the rooms were actually rather small. My wife Jill shot a movie there about ten years ago, and she walked around the house and grounds during the shoot, surprised at its modest scale. As she put it, "It was not a mansion; it was a very comfortable large house." Valentino's taste for ornate decoration made the place feel slightly crowded. On top of his taste in décor, he filled his closets with clothes—thirty business suits, ten dress suits, four riding outfits, ten overcoats, thirty-seven vests, a hundred twenty-four shirts, and on and on. His jewelry box contained thirty rings.

Falcon Lair also came equipped with all the extras—there was a stable for Valentino's four Arabian horses and a kennel for his Great Danes, Italian mastiffs, and greyhounds.

It sounds colorful and over-the-top gorgeous, but that was typical of the time. (Unfortunately, there are no surviving color photographs of the house.) Whatever their particular style, in this period and for the next quarter century it was the detailing—the materials that are often considered of peripheral importance, such as brass fittings, parchment, walnut veneers, wallpaper imported from China, whatever—that made Hollywood houses special.

It was a sybaritic environment that would have seemed over-the-top for Norma Desmond, but Valentino himself was an odd combination of aesthete and auto mechanic. His greatest pleasure, besides riding horses or playing with the dogs, involved stripping and reassembling car engines and transmissions. I've always thought that the house and its decoration must have involved a sense of performance for Valentino, but I would see that in a number of the great houses I would visit.

Valentino was making good money at this point in his life—Joe Schenck was paying him a hundred grand per picture plus a percentage of the profits (and this was in the mid-1920s!)—but there was no way he wasn't outspending his income by a factor of three or four.

When Valentino died of peritonitis in August 1926, he was deeply in debt. It was thought that Falcon Lair would sell for somewhere between $140,000 and $175,000, with his possessions worth as much as $500,000. In other words, the best-case scenario was that the house would be worth about half of what Valentino had invested in the place. If the estate hadn't been so far in the hole, it would have made sense to wait, but Valentino couldn't afford to.

When the estate auction was held, Valentino's possessions brought less than $100,000, and the house itself didn't sell at all. Finally, in 1934 an architect bought it for the minute sum of $18,000. Eventually, Doris Duke bought the house, but seldom lived in it. The majority of Falcon Lair was torn down in 2006.

The years between 1925 and the stock market crash in 1929 constituted a housing free-for-all in Beverly Hills. Spanish haciendas were built, as well as Arabian mosques, French châteaux, pueblo-inspired homes. There were even some Tudor mansions. Whatever the varying exterior styles, though, most of these houses were very modern inside, with French doors common so as to enable easy flow between indoors and the mild California outdoors.

Just as Joe Schenck had cosigned a house loan for Valentino, so Louis B. Mayer gave Joan Crawford an advance so she could buy a house on North Roxbury in Beverly Hills. The moguls thought that such loans were a good investment in rising stars they believed in, and might also provoke a feeling of gratitude that could only work to the studio's advantage. A few years later, in 1929, Crawford was an even bigger star, so Mayer OK'd a loan of forty thousand dollars so she could buy a ten-room mansion at 426 North Bristol Circle in Brentwood.

Crawford's favorite room there was the sunroom, which had windows on three sides and shelves filled with dozens of dolls—Crawford had been a deprived child and saw no reason not to pamper herself with the things she hadn't had when she was a little girl.

I heard Joan talking about how Billy Haines convinced her to get rid of her collection of hundreds of dolls and dozens of black velvet paintings of dancers. There was no way, he told her, that he could do anything to transform her house into a glamorous environment if she was going to cling to such junk. Joan valued class more than she did her collections, so she gave her dolls and paintings away.

All the prevalent architectural styles were replicated in the palatial movie theaters that were going up across the country. Some were designed as Moorish palaces with ceilings full of twinkling stars; others were Chinese, or Egyptian, but they were all wildly ornate, selling a fantasy that was way beyond the financial reach of 99 percent of the audience that flocked to them. Hollywood was embodying an oversize sense of scale that was an echo of the showmanship that was making the movies. The great sets of the silent era—Fairbanks's castle for *Robin Hood* and his even vaster sets for his Arabian Nights fantasy *The Thief of Bagdad*—provided a creative impetus for people within the movie industry and fueled the fantasies of their audiences. Why have a house when you could have a castle?

Right about this time Los Angeles also saw a proliferation of buildings whose forms imitated their functions. A ten-foot-tall orange held an orange juice stand; a huge donut housed a donut shop. There was a place called the Tail of the Pup that looked like a hot dog encased in a bun—you can guess what they sold.

The building that always intrigued me was the Utter-McKinley Mortuary on Sunset and Horn. There was a large clock mounted on top of the building, but it had no hands. Beneath it was a sign that read "24-Hour Service."

I always thought a clock without hands had a certain ominous "ask not for whom the bell tolls, it tolls for thee" significance that went far beyond undertakers, who never got a full night's sleep.

Entrepreneurs such as Sid Grauman and Max Factor had their buildings designed to resemble movie sets, and as these buildings were displayed in movies and newsreels, their styles influenced other buildings all over the world, both for and against. It's possible that without the glamorous excesses of buildings exemplified by Grauman's Chinese Theatre, the subsequent and—to my mind—overly severe architecture of Mies van der Rohe might never have happened. I suspect that Hollywood's use of dramatic, extreme architecture—and the public acceptance of it—made the world safe for the more daring architecture that later became the norm.

The studios themselves adopted the same veneer of showmanship. Some of them were more or less architecturally undistinguished factories, like Paramount. But the Chaplin studio on La

Brea was built to resemble a string of Tudor cottages, and Thomas Ince's studio in Culver City—later bought by Cecil B. DeMille and then by David Selznick—was a replica of George Washington's Mount Vernon.

And let's not overlook one of the enduring wonders of Los Angeles architecture: the Witch's House, built to house the productions of silent film director Irvin Willat. Designed by art director Harry Oliver, it was originally in Culver City but was later moved to Beverly Hills, to the corner of Carmelita Avenue and Walden Drive. Even though it's been a private residence for the last eighty years, it looks exactly like a set for *Hansel and Gretel*.

All of this exuberant eclecticism bothered the intellectuals, who thought it was vulgar. But Hollywood made its living manufacturing dreams. If it had looked like Newport, the dreams wouldn't have cascaded over the world as successfully as they did.

And one other thing: these buildings were fun to look at. They were architecture as entertainment.

When Ramon Novarro opted for a tidy house designed by Lloyd Wright, the son of Frank Lloyd Wright, he had MGM art director Cedric Gibbons redecorate entirely in black and silver. Novarro fell so in love with the look that he would ask his dinner guests to comply with the prevailing design scheme and wear only black or silver to his parties.

Gibbons was a huge influence both within the industry and without. His designs for the 1928 Joan Crawford movie *Our Dancing Daughters* showcased Art Deco throughout and helped usher out the heavy Spanish décor. Deco became the look of the young moderns—clean lines and chic.

The movie was successful enough to spawn two sequels, the last of which costarred William Haines, who didn't care for Gibbons's aesthetic and stayed away from Deco when he became a fashionable designer. "It looks like someone had a nightmare while designing a church and tried to combine it with a Grauman theater," he remarked.

In retrospect, there was a playful aspect to a lot of these houses, as if the actors, directors, and producers were extending the fantasies they created on-screen into their private lives. The houses were partly sets, partly playgrounds—literally.

Many people saw the beautiful sets designed by Cedric Gibbons at MGM or Van Nest Polglase at RKO and asked them to design their houses. Ginger Rogers had a house off Coldwater Canyon that was largely the work of Polglase. Gibbons's own house, which he designed and built for his marriage to Dolores del Río, was a stunning Moderne masterpiece. Likewise, the art director Harold Grieve, who was married to Jetta Goudal, a star for DeMille in the silent days, developed a business in interior decoration that far surpassed his work for the studios.

By 1937, when I arrived, when you got off the Pacific Electric line in Beverly Hills, nobody noticed the unpaved roads above Sunset, or the bean fields in the flats, or the modest shopping district. Everybody was mesmerized by the vastness of the homes.

When the stock market collapsed in 1929 and the Depression ensued, construction in Los Angeles also collapsed. Construction of new houses and apartments fell from 15,234 in 1929 to 6,600 in 1931. Luxury housing went into a decline, but there were plenty of available places, as silent film people who lost their footing in sound pictures had to downsize. Many of the new stars of the sound era bought secondhand homes instead of building their own, although there were exceptions. William Powell built a house with a complicated series of features that emerged from walls and rose from the floor. A bar turned into a barbecue by pushing a button; other buttons opened and closed doors. But the wiring was badly done, and there was a comic period when Powell would push a button to go into the parlor, but the kitchen door would open. The house had thirty-two rooms, and something unexpected would happen in each of them.

It would have made a great scene in a comedy starring Cary Grant—or Bill Powell—but Bill, understandably enough, didn't think it was funny.

"Follow the money" is a brief but telling sentence that has been serving reporters well since the invention of movable type. And the way we lived in Hollywood provides yet another instance of following the money.

In 1941, shortly before I started caddying at the Bel Air Country Club, two thirds of all American families earned between one thousand and three thousand dollars a year. A further 27 percent had incomes of between five hundred and one thousand dollars.

By contrast, even a middling star could reliably expect to earn as much in a week as those two thirds of American families made in a year. A lot of people on the industry's high end made many multiples of that.

So the houses, the resorts, the restaurants, the luxurious accoutrements that cluttered our lives were a direct result of the fact that, economically speaking, Hollywood wasn't like the rest of America. Not even close.

By now many businessmen and dozens of movie stars had begun

moving out of downtown Los Angeles and other old neighborhoods into the exciting nouveau riche air of Beverly Hills. Hollywood's population exploded from 36,000 in 1920 to 157,000 in 1930 and would continue to grow, but it was no longer the chic place to live.

There was a slight gap in the styles of the era; there was no smooth transition between the lavish houses of the 1920s and the more streamlined architecture of the 1930s and '40s, when architectural styles and interior decoration became noticeably less ornate and extravagant than they had been—the pendulum had swung in the opposite direction, as it always does. By the 1930s Spanish and Italian were out; neocolonial or, for particularly stylish people, Moderne, was in. One of the key transitional buildings was Union Station, which was built between 1934 and 1939, and is a beautiful example of both the Moderne and the Spanish styles—the former the new wave, the latter the old.

In this period you had Mediterranean Revival, but there were also opulent Italian Renaissance places such as Harold Lloyd's Greenacres. And then there were the polyglot palaces. The director Fred Niblo had a Spanish mansion on Angelo Drive, high above Beverly Hills, but he couldn't resist adding an English drawing room with paneling that was hundreds of years old. Period romance was all.

John Barrymore bought a comparatively modest house on Tower Road from King Vidor for fifty thousand dollars, then spent a million dollars over the next ten years on improvements. He bought an adjacent four acres, expanding the property to seven acres. He built an entirely separate Spanish house up the hill and connected the two houses with a grape arbor.

Being John Barrymore, he also had to indulge his eccentricities. Above his bedroom was a secret room that he could reach by a trapdoor and a ladder whenever he needed to get away from his family. By the entrance there was a totem pole painted red and yellow with a fern growing out of the top, like an uncombed head of hair.

By the time Barrymore was through with the project—actually, he just ran out of money—he had sixteen buildings and fifty-five rooms, with more buildings under construction. There was a skeet range, a bowling green, an aviary that held three hundred birds. It was like a little village on a mountaintop in Beverly Hills, all with red tile roofs and iron-grilled windows.

Barrymore couldn't hold on to his money—none of the Barrymores could—and by 1937 he was being pursued by the IRS for back taxes and had to declare bankruptcy. The vast estate was put up for auction, but the place was such an extension of Barrymore's idiosyncrasies and onetime income stream that no one bought it.

I never met John Barrymore, although I would have loved to have had the opportunity. I did have the good fortune to be friends with Harold Lloyd, whose house was similarly extravagant. Harold was a very special man. Greenacres, his Italian Renaissance mansion on Benedict Canyon Drive, covered twenty-two acres, forty rooms, and thirty-six thousand square feet—not counting the patios or porches.

Harold told me that by the time the house was finished in 1929, just in time for the stock market crash, he had spent two million dollars. The housewarming party began on a Friday and continued until Monday morning, with changes of bands every four hours to keep everybody energized.

Harold got what he paid for. The house had a seven-car garage and a splendid fountain by the entrance. In fact, it had *twelve* fountains, and you could hear the gurgling of water from practically every place on the property. The entrance hall itself was sixteen feet high, and there was a circular oak staircase attached to the wall without any supports beneath the risers.

Harold was particularly proud of his sunken living room, which had a coffered ceiling with gold leaf on it, elaborate paneling, and a forty-rank pipe organ for concerts or silent film accompaniment. The dining room could sit up to twenty-four guests, and the house carried a staff of thirty-two, sixteen of whom were gardeners. If you didn't want to take the stairs, an elevator could convey you to the second floor, which held ten bedrooms.

Outside, Harold built a nine-hole golf course and an Olympic-size swimming pool. There were tennis courts and handball courts and even an eight-hundred-foot-long canoe lake adjacent to the golf course. For his three children, he also built a child-size four-room

Harold Lloyd in the garden of Greenacres, his palatial Spanish-style villa in Beverly Hills.

cottage with a thatched roof, complete with electricity, plumbing, and miniature furniture.

All the furniture in the house was custom made, but Harold was from a small town in Nebraska and, believe it or not, was far from a spendthrift. Harold had a sunroom that had trompe l'oeil vines painted on the walls. The painter did a great job on the vines, and they looked quite lifelike. But he was very slow, and after a year or two the vines were still in progress. One day Harold had had enough and he told the painter he had exactly three weeks to finish the job. This explains why the small, carefully painted leaves suddenly got about five times as large in one corner of the room.

Me with Harold Lloyd's daughter Gloria, at a
costume party at Harold's Palm Springs home.

I met Harold Lloyd around 1948, when I began dating his daughter Gloria. Harold approved of the potential match, and I have to admit that his approval meant a great deal to me. At that point, Greenacres was only slightly more than twenty years old, but the upkeep on the place was huge, and Harold was no longer making a million dollars a year. He was economizing. The house had never been redecorated—the drapes were getting ragged, the furniture was frayed. Nothing had been replaced.

One year he got too busy to take down the Christmas tree, so there it stayed. Finally, he made up his mind to have a Christmas tree all year round, so each year he would install and structurally reinforce a fifteen-foot-tall tree, and then take two weeks to hang a

Harold's famous Christmas tree. I'm proud to say that somewhere in there is the ornament I gave him.

thousand ornaments out of the ten thousand he owned. It was beautiful and eccentric—but mostly beautiful. I'm very proud that one of the ornaments on the tree was a gift from me. I also had an autographed picture in what Harold called his Rogues' Gallery, a subterranean hallway lined with signed photos from everybody from Chaplin to DeMille.

Harold was one of those men who had to be busy all the time. In most respects, he was a sweet man. He was passionate about photography, passionate about the movie business. Like Fairbanks and Chaplin, Harold owned his own films, which was highly unusual for the period . . . or for any period, come to think of it.

Harold's retirement was more or less enforced by a cumulative lack of success in talking pictures, and it must have been difficult for him. He channeled all his energy into hobbies, but the problem with hobbies is that they're more about filling time than producing something that will stand through time—as Harold's films have.

But Harold kept busy. He collected old cars. He prided himself on his stereo system—the living room featured thirty-six speakers when he really cranked it up gold leaf would drift down from the ceiling like snow. Harold also became fascinated by the theory of color and started painting, and he even took up 3D photography. He ended up with more than six thousand 3D photographs. He was, in short, very interested in life. He was loyal to his staff; there were a few people he kept on salary that had been with him since the 1920s.

But in some respects, Greenacres was a strange house. Harold was consumed by his hobbies . . . and by young women. Everybody else was left to more or less fend for themselves. Mildred Davis, his wife, quietly drank. His son Harold Jr. was gay, and had a strained relationship with his father. It was a huge place for only five people, and it would have been possible to go for days without seeing anybody.

Harold died in 1971, but I retain a soft spot for both him and his unparalleled home; I shot episodes of *Switch* and *Hart to Hart* there—my way of staying in touch with my old friend. Harold's granddaughter Suzanne has shepherded Harold's movies—the most valuable part of her inheritance—with great diligence and care, so that future generations will always be able to appreciate what a great comedian and producer Harold was.

Harold, his family, and Greenacres will always be in my heart.

By the time I started going to the Beverly Hills Hotel in the late 1940s, there were already legends about the place, and there would be more in the future. Here are some that I know to be true:

Will Rogers and Spencer Tracy did play polo in what used to be a bean field behind the Polo Lounge. Clark Gable and Carole Lombard did have trysts there while waiting for his divorce to become final. "We used to go through the God-damnedest routine you ever heard of," Lombard recalled. "He'd get somebody to go hire a room or a bungalow somewhere. . . . A couple of times the Beverly Hills Hotel. . . . Then somebody would give him a key. Then he'd have another key made, and give it to me. . . . Then all the shades down and all the doors and windows locked and the phones shut off. . . . But would you believe it? After we were married, we couldn't ever make it unless we went somewhere and locked all the doors and put down all the window shades and shut off all the phones."

That was Garson Kanin reporting what Lombard had told him, and I think it's accurate until the end, when she claims that Gable had performance anxiety unless the place was locked down tight. I knew

The pool at the Beverly Hills Hotel.

Guests playing mini-golf on the grounds of the Beverly Hills Hotel.

Clark, and I can assure you that, while he would have made sure the door was locked, that would have been the extent of his paranoia.

In other romances, Marilyn Monroe and Yves Montand did carry on their affair in bungalows 20 and 21 while making *Let's*

Make Love, and Elizabeth Taylor did spend several of her honeymoons in the bungalows.

Howard Hughes kept three bungalows rented at a time. For around thirty years beginning in 1942, Bungalow 4, which had four rooms, was for Hughes's personal residence. Bungalow 19, which he kept for Jean Peters, his wife, had three rooms. (It should be mentioned that Bungalows 4 and 19 were far apart.) Bungalow 1C was for his bodyguards.

There were times when Hughes would have as many as nine of the bungalows rented, a couple of which would be occupied by girls he had signed for RKO. The rest would be empty.

He also would occasionally book the Crystal Room on thirty minutes' notice. The Crystal Room held a thousand people, but Hughes's meetings usually involved only four. Once, Hughes's Cadillac was parked at the hotel for two years without ever being moved. The tires all gradually flattened, but nobody inflated them and nobody moved the car.

Were any average hotel guest to leave his Cadillac on the grounds to deteriorate, the car would be towed and the owner would be presented with the bill. But Hughes was too good a customer for the hotel to take any such drastic measures.

By 1948, Hughes's injuries from his Beverly Hills plane crash were beginning to overwhelm him. He would stay inside Bungalow 4 for months at a time. I remember the staff at the hotel mulling over Hughes's eccentricities—the way he would order roast beef sandwiches (the hotel went so far as to designate a "roast beef man," who was the only one who had been able to master Hughes's careful instructions about how to prepare them) accompanied by pineapple upside-down cake. He would tell the staff to stick the sandwiches in a tree, then retrieve them when nobody was around, so no one would know in which bungalow he was staying. He also liked Hershey chocolate bars and Poland Spring water.

In 1949 John Steinbeck met his last wife at the Beverly Hills Hotel. He was in town working on *Viva Zapata!* and a friend offered to fix him up with Ava Gardner. Gardner wasn't interested, so the friend fixed him up with Ann Sothern instead. They hit it off, and he invited her to visit him in Monterey. She brought along a friend named Elaine Scott, who was married to Zachary Scott. But not for long—Steinbeck and Elaine hit it off to such an extent that both Ann Sothern and Zachary Scott faded into the distance. Supposedly Sothern never forgave Steinbeck . . . and quite probably never forgave Elaine Steinbeck, either.

Other bungalows had other famous guests. Bungalow 5 was the favorite of Elizabeth Taylor and Richard Burton, and Paul and Linda McCartney liked it as well. Bungalow 9 was the home of Jennifer Jones and Norton Simon for five years. Bungalow 11 sheltered Marlene Dietrich for three years, including her custom-made seven-by-eight-foot bed. Bungalows 14 to 21 were known as "Bachelors Row," and were the favorites of Warren Beatty and Orson Welles among many others.

By the 1950s, the Beverly Hills Hotel was synonymous with Beverly Hills itself. But in fact, in 1933 the hotel had closed because of the Depression and stood vacant for two years, until the Bank of America reopened it a year later.

In 1942 the hotel was purchased by Hernando Courtright, who was a vice president at the Bank of America. He had no experience in the hotel business, but he knew a good opportunity when he saw one, so he raised one hundred thousand dollars from Harry

Rita Hayworth posing poolside at the Beverly Hills Hotel.

Warner, Irene Dunne, and Loretta Young*—notice the pedigrees. Then he borrowed another seventy-five thousand dollars to remodel the place.

That same year Courtright rechristened the El Jardin Restaurant the Polo Lounge to pay tribute to demon polo enthusiasts Will Rogers, Tommy Hitchcock, and Darryl Zanuck—and as such it's been more or less constantly successful ever since. Toward the end

---

* It's not generally known, but Gladys Belzer, Loretta Young's mother, had a thriving career as a decorator to the Hollywood set; she often collaborated with the architect John Woolf, who built houses for Fanny Brice, among many others.

of the decade, Hernando gave the place its first major redecoration. In 1947 he opened the Crystal Room and the Lanai Restaurant, which later became the Coterie.

Courtright's wife, Firenza, described what he accomplished: "He had a business side and a social side and his business was hospitality. He was a showman, setting the stage for each visitor. He had a great sense of style and, as well, an extra effort to push himself harder than anybody else. In many ways, running [the] hotel was like running a small country."

Hernando also broadened the number of amenities available at the hotel. Francis Taylor, the father of Elizabeth, opened an art gallery in the downstairs shopping area in 1939, and through the war years the Francis Taylor Gallery became an increasingly important venue for art. Francis sold a lot of California Impressionists, such as Granville Redmond (a deaf artist who had a studio at the Chaplin lot on La Brea for a number of years and who also appeared in some of Chaplin's films). Francis also sold work by Augustus John. His prices were reasonable, so actors who were also discerning collectors, such as Vincent Price, James Mason, and Greta Garbo, purchased a lot of art from him.

Interestingly, although its "Pink Palace" moniker may seem as old as the hotel itself, the hotel wasn't actually painted that color until 1948 under the direction of Paul Revere Williams, who also designed the customized cursive script for its logo. Williams was a very dignified, classy man who was born in 1894 and who encountered all the discrimination you might expect would face a young black man in that era. "I determined, when I was still in high school, to become an architect," said Williams. "When I announced my intention to my instructor, he stared at me with as much astonishment as he would have displayed had I proposed a rocket flight to Mars. 'Who ever heard of a Negro being an architect?' he demanded."

Williams knew that he was going to have to depend almost entirely on white clients, so his first impression had to be faultless. Paul was light skinned, always impeccably dressed, and had taught himself to draw upside down. As soon as a client sat down with him, Paul would start sketching out the plans upside down, which would quickly disarm anyone who was taken aback by the fact that his architect was black. And then Paul would ask for suggestions, and the customer would become a full partner in the project. Brilliant psychology.

In 1949 Williams created the new Crescent Wing, which added 109 rooms to the hotel, and turned it from a T plan to an H plan. Also overhauled were the Polo Lounge and the Fountain Coffee Shop, and the lobby took on its timeless pink and green color scheme that's been maintained ever since.

The pink and green banana leaf wallpaper, however, was actually the work of Don Loper, who made his name as a dress designer for, among many others, Marilyn Monroe.

It's a mark of how brilliant Paul's design for the Polo Lounge was that his is the only hot spot I can think of that has survived unchanged from 1949 to the present day.

Paul is an example of the remarkable openness of Los Angeles to the new, the untried in architecture and style. I think this was possible because you had a set of circumstances that weren't replicated anyplace else in the country: a basically thriving local economy, a large group of talented architects, and—most important—clients who were interested in anything theatrical or new.

When I started going to the Polo Lounge in the late forties, it wasn't terribly expensive by Hollywood standards—a daiquiri might cost you seventy-five cents, but a Pimm's would run more than a dollar and a bottle of Mumm's Cordon Rouge champagne from 1929 would set you back more than twenty dollars. So the tourists stayed away simply by dint of the tabs.

Paul Williams had completed all his additions to the hotel by the time Stanley Anderson died in 1951. Stanley was one of the pioneers of Southern California, but outside of his participation in the birth of Beverly Hills and the hotel that bears the town's name, he's not remembered by many people. But he's very much remembered by me.

Hernando Courtright sold the place in 1953 for $5.5 million, and by that time the Beverly Hills Hotel was the premier hotel in the area. He continued managing the place for a couple of years, but he didn't like the new owner, a man from Detroit named Ben Silberstein. And then things got really interesting: Hernando's wife left him for Silberstein. Courtright then took over the Beverly Wilshire, which he ran very successfully until he sold it a year before his death in 1986.

Hernando Courtright was a good man and a wonderful hotelier. He really knew how to run a place, and he ran it beautifully. Scandals, whether on the part of the guests or the staff, happened mostly out of range of the newspapers, and completely out of range of the guests. The atmosphere was smooth and utterly unruffled. As far as the public was concerned, the Beverly Hills Hotel was the chicest place in town. The Duke and Duchess of Windsor would stay there when they were in town, as would Princess Margaret and Lord Snowdon. When Charlie Chaplin came back to Hollywood in 1972 to accept an honorary Oscar, he stayed at the Beverly Hills Hotel. A lot of the people went there for Hernando as much as they did anything else. When you drove down to the hotel and went into the Polo Lounge to have a drink, it was different than going to any other place in town.

Hernando's great innovation was psychological. In his view,

Beverly Hills was not a resort area, nor even a suburb: it was up-town Los Angeles. Hernando wanted to make the town the equivalent of Fifth Avenue in New York or Worth Avenue in Palm Beach, and the Beverly Hills Hotel was, you might say, the anchor store—the prestige destination in a town full of them.

Today, the twenty-two bungalows are set amid lush tropical gardens, with private walkways that snake through groves of coconut palms, oleanders, and bougainvillea. The landscaping is dense in order to give the bungalow inhabitants the privacy they desire, and often need.

The bungalows, which are basically tile-roofed mini-haciendas, have "privacy lights" instead of "Do Not Disturb" signs. They all have fireplaces, full kitchens, and fresh orchids in the bathrooms. Some bungalows have two or three bedrooms, others four.

Since 1987, the Sultan of Brunei has owned both the Beverly Hills Hotel and the Hotel Bel Air, and you may make of that what you will. The sultan is an oilman, but he also loves to play polo, so in that respect the ghost of Hernando Courtright should be pleased, although as far as I'm concerned it's outsourcing gone berserk.

The Beverly Hills Hotel is emblematic of the best aspects of the town it anchors. People who don't know any better think the movie business and, by extension, America, has always been just one thing, permanent and unalterable, but the closer you look at history, the more you realize that everything that lasts—like, for instance, the Beverly Hills Hotel—has been reinvented numerous times and by numerous people.

When men like Hernando die, there's a loss of great personalities, not to mention a loss of history. No matter how well a corporation runs a hotel or a restaurant, the personal touch is gone.

Just one example: They took out the tennis courts at the Beverly Hills Hotel, so the two men who ran them for years, Alex Olmedo and his brother, David, also disappeared. Alex was a joy, a Peruvian who won four NCAA titles and played on the Davis Cup team for America. Kate Hepburn took lessons from Alex, as did Robert Duvall and Chevy Chase.

Bill Tilden taught there. Many wonderful people went to those courts. It was a little piece of Hollywood history, but, like so much of Hollywood history, it's gone.

Just about the time I arrived in Hollywood, if you rode down the ramp from Ocean Avenue to Santa Monica, Marion Davies's palace—I don't use the word lightly—was just off to the right, and the beach houses of Harold Lloyd, Norma Shearer, Louis B. Mayer, and Jesse Lasky were farther on in that direction. To the left off the ramp were Leo McCarey, George Bancroft, and Norma Talmadge, and a couple of places owned by Ben Lyon and Bebe Daniels.

Norma Talmadge's place at 1038 Ocean Front had a particularly distinguished list of inhabitants. Randolph Scott and Cary Grant had lived there in the mid-thirties, and Cary had kept the place when he married Barbara Hutton. After that, Brian Aherne lived there; Howard Hughes rented the place for a time, as did Grace Kelly. Roman Polanski and Sharon Tate lived there as well. Douglas Fairbanks was a couple of doors down in a house he had initially bought as a weekend getaway, but converted to his full-time residence after his divorce from Mary Pickford.

Norma Talmadge is forgotten today, which is sad, because she was a fine emotional actress, and one of the three or four biggest female stars of the silent era. (The reason nobody remembers her is that very few of her films survive.)

When she built the place in the late 1920s, she was married to Joe Schenck. I've always wondered whether the Norman design of the house was an elaborate pun on her name. The interior was decorated mostly in a Spanish motif, although Norma's bathroom was done with tiles from Malibu Pottery, which was among the most beautiful work ever done in that medium. Interestingly, Norma had almost nothing in her house that indicated she was a movie star, other than a portrait of her over the fireplace in the living room.

Norma lived there for about five years, after which she divorced Schenck and took up with Gilbert Roland, a good friend of mine in later years. Gil always regarded Norma as the great love of his life, which, for a compulsive ladies' man, is really saying something.

Although Norma's career ended after only two sound pictures, she had held on to her money—something that couldn't be said of a lot of silent film stars. She had two other beachfront properties in Santa Monica, as well as other real estate investments around Los Angeles.

These Santa Monica and Malibu houses—always excluding Marion Davies's place, which could have sheltered an army—looked quite modest. They still do—most of them are still there, although they've been heavily altered over the years. Most of them were a complete change of pace from the Spanish influence that was predominant in Hollywood. Some derived from Cape Cod style; others reflected a Newport or Monterey influence.

If Hollywood was prone to strange fads—the famously arrogant director Josef von Sternberg had a house designed by Richard Neutra in Chatsworth that looked like an aluminum pillbox that just

happened to have a moat around it—it had an even stranger love of
huge parties, as if in defiance of the Depression. Hearst loved to
throw dos at San Simeon, but also at Marion Davies's huge house in
Santa Monica, which the naive often assumed was a resort hotel.
Actually, it was the only competition Harold Lloyd had for the
most lavish movie star estate.

The Santa Monica beach house was by no means Marion's pri-
mary residence. That was actually a Spanish-style mansion at 1700
Lexington Road in Beverly Hills. The Beverly Hills house was
Marion's preferred venue for parties, simply because the Santa
Monica house was too damn big—it could supposedly hold two
thousand guests, which sounds more like Buckingham Palace than
Santa Monica, but then Marion's place wasn't much smaller than
Buckingham Palace.

There was a small-town atmosphere in Hollywood then. One or
two nights a week, Davies would invite a few close friends to her
place. Since her close friends were named Chaplin and Fairbanks,
it may sound like an intimidating evening, but the evenings mostly
consisted of dinner and charades. A few weeks later, Chaplin or
Fairbanks would return the favor. Sometimes Marion would hire a
bus, fill it with ten or twenty friends, plenty of food, maybe a musician or two, and take off for Santa Monica beach, where they would
have a late picnic and a bonfire.

William Randolph Hearst built the Santa Monica palace for Davies in 1928, the last, flamboyant year of the silent era. Money was
clearly no object. The house held down 750 feet of oceanfront real
estate—and this at a time when anything more than fifty feet was
regarded as a luxury. Hearst assembled the land piecemeal, using
various pseudonyms in order to keep the prices down.

The story goes that the last parcel of the property belonged to

Will Rogers, which Hearst wanted for the tennis court. The land was worth about five thousand dollars, but Rogers found out who the buyer really was. By the time they were through negotiating, Rogers got a hundred thousand dollars for his parcel.

To give you some idea of the scale of Davies's place, it had five buildings, a hundred ten rooms, fifty-five bathrooms, and thirty-seven antique fireplaces. For one party in 1937, to which I was unaccountably not invited, they installed a merry-go-round on the grounds.

The Beach House was small only in comparison to Hearst's San Simeon, which was situated on 240,000 acres. But you couldn't make movies and commute from San Simeon, so Hearst simply built his mistress an equivalent in Santa Monica. While the exterior was Neocolonial in design, inside it was eclectic. There were vast rooms on the first floor, a ballroom, a theater, dozens of bedrooms on the second floor—a random succession of grand rooms that had no connection to one another.

As with San Simeon, Hearst's decorating principle was simple: he bought entire rooms out of various European castles and installed them in Davies's new house. The dining room, drawing room, and reception hall came from Burton Hall in Ireland. Then there was a ballroom from an eighteenth-century Venetian palazzo. A tavern in the basement had been a pub in the Elizabethan era, and sat fifty. Davies herself lived on the top floor of the main building, with a spectacular view that looked out to sea and up the coast.

There's a story that gives you some idea of the scale on which Hearst and Davies lived. It seems that Davies had ordered a twenty-four-by-one-hundred-foot custom rug for the movie theater on the second floor. After misadventures with the shipping, the rug finally

Everett Collection

The beach-side facade of Marion Davies's Santa Monica home, known as Ocean-house.

arrived, and it was found that there was no possible way it could be brought inside the house.

No problem. Davies simply ordered part of the wall to be removed; then the rug was lifted into the house by crane, and the wall was rebuilt. It sounds like the type of, well, off-the-wall thing that today would be done only by Arab sheikhs residing in Dubai. In that era, Hollywood *was* Dubai.

The Beach House was a popular site for theme parties—Pioneer Days, or Tyrolean, or whatever incongruous thing they could dream up. One time Davies threw what she called a "Baby Party," for which all the guests had to dress up as children. Joan Crawford came as Shirley Temple, while Clark Gable made an appearance as a Boy Scout. (It was an echo of a similar party in the 1920s, when

Alla Nazimova appeared in diapers and Wallace Reid came as Buster Brown.) Perhaps the most creative party involved an invitation demanding that couples arrive wearing exactly what they had on when their romance began. Lee Tracy and his wife came in a shower curtain.

Once, Norma Shearer showed up as Marie Antoinette for a party billed as all-American. Norma's hoop skirt was so huge that seats had to be removed from her car before she could get in.

Davies was a good-natured woman, greatly loved by everybody who knew her, but Shearer was a thorn in her side. Like Joan Crawford and most of the other actresses on the MGM lot, she was jealous of Shearer's ability to land film roles simply because she was married to Irving Thalberg. And now this.

Davies told Shearer she'd have to take off the dress if she wanted to enter the party. The two women got into it, but Shearer got her way. Hearst may have been running a publishing empire, but Irving Thalberg ran production at MGM, where Marion was making her movies.

And that wasn't even Shearer's most aggressive look-at-me display. Hedda Hopper once told me about a party that Carole Lombard threw. It was supposed to be a white ball—nothing but white gowns on the women. The event was to be held at the restaurant Victor Hugo—the perfect setting for such a lavish display. Norma came late, as was her wont, but that wasn't what proved so devastating: she was wearing a bright red gown.

It was all a reenactment of the climactic scene in Bette Davis's *Jezebel*, but the people at the party weren't amused. Shearer had gone far out of her way to show up the hostess, and that was simply bad form. Like Marion Davies, Carole Lombard had a widespread reputation for being a salt of the earth dame, but she was livid and stormed out, followed closely by Clark Gable.

I went to school with Norma's son, Irving Thalberg Jr., who brought me over to the house one day to meet her. She was in bed, where Irving had led me to believe she spent a great deal of her time, resting up so she could look radiant at parties. She was sweet, and signed a still for me, which I still have. But stories like the one Hedda Hopper told me indicate that to get between Norma Shearer and something she wanted would have been a very bad idea.

Marion Davies lived at Beach House until World War II. At that point Hearst became worried about a Japanese invasion. Don't laugh—there was a great deal of fear in California about just such a possibility. Spielberg's *1941* wasn't much of a movie, but it was based on fact. Davies moved back to San Simeon and her house in Beverly Hills. But because she disliked San Simeon—she thought it was gloomy—she spent most of her time in Beverly Hills. Years later, long after Davies had died, that house became famous when it was used as the location for the home of the movie producer played by John Marley in *The Godfather*. A horse's head in Marion Davies's old bedroom!

Hearst's empire contracted radically during the Depression and afterward. Part of it was the economy, and part of it was that he was extremely conservative at a time when the dominant philosophy was the New Deal. He couldn't afford both places, so the Beach House was sold for six hundred thousand dollars—which might have paid for one of the ballrooms—and he held on to San Simeon.

In 1947 Beach House became a hotel, called Oceanhouse, but the venture failed and the main house was demolished in 1956; three years later the property was sold to the state of California. All that's left of one of the great mansions of California's past is one guest-house, which had been used by Davies's family. Still later the property was taken over by Wallis Annenberg, who turned it into a public community center. I've gone there with my grandson Riley, holding his hand and reflecting on the vast palace that once stood on the spot. Someday, when he's old enough, I'll tell him all about it.

Small beach cottages helped launch the decorating career of Billy Haines. Haines had opened an antiques shop in 1930 while he was still under contract with MGM. He had an innate understanding of his potential market; Hollywood had attracted thousands of people from all over the world, most with very limited educations but with boundless ambitions. They needed to be led, but gently. The antiques shop displayed Haines's antiques in complete room settings, so that people without the gift of visualization could see what the chairs or couches or vases would look like in context. And of course it also allowed Haines to sell extra pieces, and sometimes entire room ensembles.

After his acting career ended, Ben Lyon became the head of talent at 20th Century Fox. Ben told me that it was he and his wife Bebe Daniels—not Joan Crawford—who had given Haines his first commission as a decorator.

Lyon had a cottage with about thirty feet of beach frontage, and he told Haines to make it sufficiently attractive so they could rent it for extra income. Haines enclosed the porch, making it part of the living room, and decorated everything in red, white, and blue. His bill for everything, including the furniture, was twenty-five hundred dollars.

Because Haines had been a star himself, he had an intimate

understanding of a star's mentality and a star's needs. Basically, he made them feel special. Plus he knew how to gain a star's trust—perhaps the most valuable quality a designer (or, for that matter, a director) can have.

Once Haines was done redecorating Carole Lombard's house, the drawing room featured six shades of blue velvet and Empire furniture. Her bedroom had an oversize bed in plum-covered satin, with mirrored screens at either side. The dining room had satin curtains that trailed on the floor. The result was every bit as sleek as Lombard herself, and totally feminine. That was the way Carole lived until she married Clark Gable, who would have felt out of place in such surroundings.

Haines did Lombard's and Joan Crawford's houses for free, as a favor to friends, figuring that the Hollywood scuttlebutt would bring customers to his door.

In 1935, he moved his shop to Sunset Boulevard, quite close to all his prospective clients in Beverly Hills. I remember driving by Haines's imposing double-doored entrance hundreds of times over the years. On either side of the doors were large glass niches with oversize glass vitrines.

Very posh.

Haines's next big commission was George Cukor's house. "It looks just like a Hollywood director's home ought to look," said Cukor when he beheld the results.

In 1934 Frank Lloyd Wright declared that California's "eclectic procession to and fro in the rag-tag and cast-off of the ages was never going to stop." This was his way of declaring defeat; he had been trying to class up the joint by designing several homes in the area:

the Hollyhock House and three other concrete-block Mayan-style houses, designed and built between 1919 and 1924. They're splendid examples of Wright's midcareer style—and they're all still standing—but they only added to the stylistic confusion of LA.

Hollyhock House is located at the corner of Sunset and Vermont—not known as a particularly great neighborhood now, but in 1919, when ground was broken, it was virgin territory. It was commissioned by Aline Barnsdall as a home that would overlook an artist's colony and theater complex. Wright was always juggling multiple projects, so when construction began he was spending a great deal of time in Tokyo, where he was designing the Imperial Hotel. While Wright was traveling, so was Barnsdall, and the distance bred a lot of disagreements, which only increased when they met face-to-face.

"How can you put a door there?" she'd yell. "I don't like it and I won't have it. Change it!"

"No!" Wright would yell right back. "That's the way it's going to be! I won't change it."

She'd insist, and he would go ahead and do what he wanted to do. It was like a bad marriage. The upshot was that Barnsdall lived in the house only for a year, after which she offered it to the city as a public park and art center.

While all this was going on, Los Angeles was exploding in all directions. The population had grown from 576,673 in 1920 to 1.2 million in 1930. Four hundred thousand of those people had arrived in the space of just five years. All those newcomers had to live somewhere, and the Southern California real estate boom was quite probably the largest and most loosely managed in history.

Meanwhile, areas farther west, such as Brentwood and Pacific

property, and Jack built a bridge between the two properties so guests could play eighteen if they so desired.

The interesting thing about Jack's estate—"house" doesn't begin to cover it—was that Jack put it together piece by piece over a ten-year period. He originally bought three acres in 1926 and built a fifteen-room Spanish mansion. But three acres felt insufficient, so Jack added another parcel of land, and then another.

The grounds were completed in 1937, at which point Jack turned his attention to his house. He hired Roland Coate to enlarge and completely redesign the old Spanish mansion into a new Georgian mansion, and Coate went to town on the assignment.

When he was done, besides the house itself and the guesthouses, there were gas pumps and a garage where repairs could be done on Jack's fleet of cars. But everybody agreed that the pièce de résistance was the golf course. The holes were on the short side—pitch and putt, really—but that wasn't the point. The point was that Jack had enough power and money to customize a golf course on some of the most valuable real estate in the world.

If you didn't already know that Jack was a rich and powerful man, the entrance to his mansion would have told you. Past the iron gates was a winding driveway lined by sycamores. You ended up at a brick-paved motor court by the portico—all white and classical. Across the way was a fountain, and beyond that were landscaped terraces decorated with statues and urns.

Needless to say, the interior of the mansion maintained the same impression of grandeur. Jack hired William Haines to do the decoration. Haines liked big houses.

Billy filled the house with antiques befitting the setting—authentic George III mahogany armchairs, writing desks, eighteenth-century Chinese wallpaper panels. (At this stage of his career, Haines liked French and English antiques with chinoiserie accents—a weird kind of Regency effect. In later years, he modernized his style to something more aerodynamic and Scandinavian looking.)

The front door opened into a two-story hall with a parquet floor. Sweeping up the side was a curving cantilevered staircase. On the wall as you ascended the staircase were paintings by Arcimboldo, the eccentric artist—well, *I've* always thought he was eccentric—who made portraits out of fruit and vegetables.

The library was where Jack spent the most time, because it had been converted into a screening room where he watched movies with his executives. When you twisted the head of a Buddha, paintings would rise and a screen would emerge.

The library, which also held a collection of scripts from Warner Bros. films, was largely decorated in orange, from the couches to the curtains. Because of the color scheme and the low furniture—so heads wouldn't get in the way of the projector's beam—it had a more modern feel than the rest of the house, except for some Louis XV–style panels that broke up the walls and drapes.

Somewhere in the house over a mantel, I recall a portrait of Ann Warner painted by Salvador Dalí. The bar had a large wooden floor and more orange accents, with Tang dynasty pottery and a couple of huge candlesticks that I seem to recall came from a Mexican cathedral. Behind the bar were statues of the Buddhist deity Guanyin, which Ann had insisted reappear in various places throughout the house.

I always wanted to ask Jack what he thought about Buddhism. Maybe he figured a little Buddhism on the side amounted to hedging his bets, but the truth is I don't think Jack Warner ever believed in anything except Jack Warner.

Overall, the house was more like an architectural museum than a place you'd actually want to live. When you had the privilege of dining at Jack's house, the silverware wasn't silver but gold, and a footman stood behind every diner at the table.

Ann Warner was a very upbeat lady, vivacious and full of life, even though theirs was a difficult marriage. In the silent days, she and Jack had had an affair, which eventually resulted in his divorcing his first wife and her divorcing her husband Don Alvarado, one of the many actors who vied for Rudolph Valentino's public after Valentino died. (To give you some idea of the incestuous nature of Hollywood, Don Alvarado later went to work for Jack at Warner Bros., using the name Don Page.)

Ann had at least one other serious affair after that, with Eddie Albert. As for Jack, monogamy was not part of the marital deal as he understood it. Yet he was mortally afraid of his wife. I've never understood why, but there it is. Whatever their private compromises, they stayed married for the rest of their lives.

There was an intense clannishness on the part of the Warners. For that matter, that same clannishness played a part in the character of almost all the men who formed Hollywood. That, and an extreme competitiveness.

For instance: In the 1950s, Jack euchred his brother Harry out of the studio. Jack had suggested to Harry that they sell out and retire to enjoy their families and the fruits of their labors. TV had rolled in, the audience was declining, they were both getting older, and it wasn't fun anymore. The argument was convincing, and Harry went along with it.

But Jack was bluffing—he had no intention of retiring. After their combined shares were sold to financier Serge Semenenko, Jack bought back all the shares in a prearranged sweetheart deal. (Semenenko had a coarseness all his own; my wife Natalie once told me that when she met Semenenko for the first time, he stuck his tongue down her throat. Even Jack wasn't that crude.)

Warner Bros. was now the sole possession of Jack Warner. Harry had a stroke soon afterward and was never the same man. When Harry finally died, Jack didn't go to the funeral, but then he probably would not have been welcome. Sixty-odd years later, Harry's side of the family rarely, if ever, speaks to Jack's side of the family.

Clan loyalty dies hard.

I played a lot of tennis at Jack's house. The tennis court was professionally lit, so you could play at any hour of the night. He didn't look like it, and God knows he didn't act like it, but Jack was a very good tennis player, as was Solly Baiano, his executive in charge of talent. But you had to be wary of Jack on the court—his calls about a ball being in or out of bounds could be highly questionable.

Did Jack cheat? I wouldn't put it like that. But I would say that his competitive nature led him to make consistently dubious decisions. Let's just say that after playing tennis with Jack Warner, you had an increased respect for what Bette Davis, Errol Flynn, and Jimmy Cagney had to go through for all those years.

After Jack died in 1978, Ann stayed on at the house until her death in 1990. At that point, David Geffen purchased the estate and the furnishings for $47.5 million. Jack's house was the last entirely intact estate to be sold in Beverly Hills, and the money Geffen paid set a national record for a single-family residence.

Geffen is a man of taste, so I'm sure he's maintained it as Jack and Ann would have wanted, but somehow I can't imagine that house without those two around to liven it up.

In stark contrast to Jack's house was that of Lew Wasserman, the head of MCA Universal. Lew was of a different generation than Jack and had very different politics—Lew was a Democrat, while Jack was a conservative Republican—so it's not surprising that he had a very different temperament as well. If he liked you, he was warm and accommodating, but to those people toward whom he was indifferent, or simply in business with, Lew could be one cold fish.

Lew's house was quite modern, and was an authentic reflection of his personality. It featured stark lines, but also art that he understood, including paintings by Vlaminck and lots of Impressionists. Lew would usually entertain at Chasen's, but he would also occasionally invite guests to his home. In either case black tie was called for, because that's the sort of couple that Lew and Edie Wasserman were.

Interestingly, the homes of the great movie moguls didn't seem to have much direct relationship to their personalities as reflected in the movies they made. The contrast between Jack Warner's house and Jack's films, for example, was staggering. Warner Bros. movies typically featured snarling mugs like Cagney, Bogart, and Eddie Robinson and tough women like Bette Davis, but his home was the height of rarified style. If I had to take a guess, I would say that his movies represented Jack as he actually was—dapper, energetic, and cracking cheap jokes—and the house represented him as he wished to be.

Joe Schenck ran United Artists and was the chairman of 20th Century Fox. Yiddish has a word for Joe Schenck: *haimish*. Joe was a rabbi to everybody in the movie business. He was round, unassuming, unpretentious, and wise.

After Norma Talmadge divorced him because she was having an affair with Gilbert Roland (later, she would marry George Jessel—there's no accounting for taste), Joe built a neoclassical mansion on South Carolwood Drive, just west of Beverly Hills. There he spent the rest of his life entertaining beautiful young women, including Marilyn Monroe. Joe died in 1961, and subsequent owners of the house included Tony Curtis and Sonny and Cher.

Darryl Zanuck, who gave me my career, built one of the last great homes to be constructed along the Santa Monica stretch of beach. Darryl's movies were evenly divided between light entertainments in garish Technicolor (such as Betty Grable's films), grim film noirs (*Nightmare Alley, Call Northside 777*), and westerns that could have been film noirs (*My Darling Clementine, The Ox-Bow Incident*). Darryl was always an innovator, a ceaselessly active man—I can barely remember him standing still.

Darryl's house at Santa Monica beach, 546 Ocean Front, was a three-story white clapboard house that could have been transplanted intact from New England or upstate New York. Darryl and his wife Virginia Fox hired Wallace Neff to design the house; when the job was finished in 1937, Virginia hired Cornelia Conger to do the interiors.

You would never know that it was the home of one of the most dynamic moguls of his time, for there was nothing theatrical about it. Virginia's collection of Staffordshire dogs and English china was displayed over the fireplace, and the whole house had a restrained English feel to it. The furniture was Chippendale and Old English, the wallpapers were hand painted—Virginia had excellent, refined tastes.

I suppose you could characterize the style of the Santa Monica beach house as predominantly Virginia's, but Ric-Su-Dar, Darryl's other residence (which he named after his children, Richard, Susan,

Darryl F. Zanuck's Santa Monica beach house.

and Darrylin), in Palm Springs, was not really any more in keeping with his own personal style—which was, in a word, swashbuckling. Darryl was a man's man, a ladies' man, and extremely competitive at everything to which he turned his hand.

Darryl raised his family at the Santa Monica house, and some of his favorite employees were nearby—Ernst Lubitsch, for one, had a place a little farther down the Pacific Coast Highway. It was a perfect place for entertaining, and Virginia hosted many elegant Sunday afternoon buffets. She was a very gracious woman—that seems to have been a job requirement for the wives of the moguls—and I liked her tremendously.

The house at 546 Ocean Front clearly meant a lot to the Zanucks. Darryl's son Richard—who used to be handed over to me to babysit, and who grew up to be a great producer in his own right—eventually bought the house from his mother and lived there for years with his own family.

Dick Zanuck was a remarkable man in so many ways—the obstacles he had to overcome in order to carve out his niche! He once told me the story of how he took over Fox. It was after *The Longest Day*, and the studio was in the doldrums. Dick went to Paris to be with his father, who was thinking of coming back and taking over the studio . . . again.

"You know all these young people," Darryl told him. "Do you know anybody who could run production? Here's what I want you to do. At dinner tonight, bring me a list of people who could run the studio."

That night, Dick handed his father a note. On it was just one word: "Me." And that was the beginning of Dick's reign as a studio head.

Dick sold 546 Ocean Front some years before he died in 2012, but I'll always remember it as the Zanuck house. And Darryl and Dick Zanuck will always be in my heart.

Me with my young friend Richard Zanuck and his first wife, Lili.

✳

As my own career began to flourish and I began circulating among my fellow movie stars in areas full of money, I encountered a number of surprises. For instance, James Cagney's house on Coldwater Canyon.

The house itself looked like an unpretentious Connecticut farmhouse. It had two stories—the exterior of the first story was finished in fieldstone, the second floor in shingles.

It was not large, with only six or seven markedly small rooms, and a warm, rustic interior. Jim's study was very masculine, with roughly finished boards, lots of books, a card table, and a piano. The house had been completed just before World War II, and that's where Jim lived when he was making a movie in town. Otherwise, he was in the east, at either of his farms in Dutchess County or on Martha's Vineyard.

The Beverly Hills house wasn't exactly a cottage, but it seemed incomprehensible as a residence for a great star like Cagney. But then Jim wasn't your typical great star. He always felt that Jack Warner was taking advantage of him, but he was never really successful away from the studio. He broke away a couple of times— once, briefly, in the thirties, and later, during the war and after, when he set up Cagney Productions with his brother Bill.

But the pictures Jim made for himself showcased him not as his fans wanted to see him—snarling, taking on the cops and the world with a gun in his hand—but as he wanted to see himself: in literary material such as *Johnny Come Lately* or *The Time of Your Life*, in which he played a quiet, reflective man in transition. Those pictures would disappoint, and he would troop back to Warner, grumbling the entire time.

There were very few personal touches in Jim's Hollywood house. One of them was a track that he had constructed right on Coldwater Canyon—his property encompassed ten acres—where I would jog his trotters when I was a teenager. I got the job through the Dornan family, who were good friends of his. There weren't a lot of grooms around Hollywood at that point, so I lucked into the job.

I was just a kid at that point, so he didn't have to be nice to me, but he always was. That's the kind of man Jim Cagney was. He liked people, he was very open, and he was very compassionate about animals. If you cared about animals, Jim was your friend. Since I was young and loved horses, I was one of his people. Ten years later, I died in his arms in *What Price Glory*—one of the great thrills of my life.

Inside Jimmy's house was a dance studio with a wooden floor and a record player where Jimmy would practice, either to make sure he could still do the steps he'd been doing since his days as a chorus boy in New York or to lose weight for a movie. Dance was Jimmy's main exercise.

There were never any parties at Jimmy's home; he and his wife kept to themselves, and I don't remember him socializing much at all, except for the occasional night out with the Irish mafia—Pat O'Brien, Frank McHugh, etc.

Jim never displayed much affection for the town of Hollywood— he seemed to regard it as a necessary evil, the financial basis for his real identity as a horse breeder and farmer—but he kept that house to the end of his life. Every winter, when the weather back east got nasty, he and his wife would come back to California and get in touch with their small circle of friends. It was something of a pain— Jim wouldn't fly, so they had to drive across the country—but by that time the Coldwater Canyon home had become a refuge for an elderly couple.

Men like Jim didn't usually hop around when it came to real estate. Likewise Fred Astaire—he built his house in 1960, some six years after his beloved wife Phyllis had died, and he lived in it for the rest of his life with his daughter Ava and his mother. When Ava left home to get married and his mother died, he lived there with a housekeeper. And he continued living there after he married Robyn Smith in 1980, until he died seven years later.

Fred's home was tastefully done, but not what you might expect—classy, but in a slightly bloodless way. It had designer written all over it, which I suspect was a function of Phyllis's not being around to personalize it. In addition to books, the library had Fred's Oscar and his Emmys, but it also had a pool table and a backgammon table. Over the fireplace was a portrait of one of Fred's prize racehorses. (Half the people in my life have loved horses; the other half have loved dogs.) The dining room was done in period English furniture and Georgian silver.

Fred's artwork was particularly interesting, as most of it had been done by friends or family rather than by professional artists. Over a cabinet in the dining room was a painting by Ava, and Cecil Beaton had contributed a painting of Fred's beloved sister Adele. I remember a couple of paintings of birds that had been done by Irving Berlin. They were quietly witty and charming, just like their owner.

In thinking about those times, I've realized that the watchword for the Hollywood lifestyle then was "diversity." Whatever one's taste in either people or houses, it could be met. My friend Cliff May was one of the men who saw to the latter. Cliff was the primary practitioner of what would come to be known as the California ranch house. Beginning in the early 1930s and continuing until his death in 1989, Cliff designed more than eighteen thousand ranch houses all over America and as far away as Australia.

Cliff looked like a cowboy. He was slender and handsome, with pale grayish eyes, sandy hair, and an ambling walk. And to his dying day he loved the ladies.

He was a sixth-generation San Diegan, born in 1908. When he was a boy, he would summer at his aunt's Monterey-style adobe in Santa Margarita, but the influence didn't immediately take. Cliff never studied architecture; rather, he was a musician—a saxophone player. His father thought music was a ridiculous business and nudged him to do something else. That something else turned into various pursuits—piloting, horses, many other things.

In 1931 he left San Diego State without graduating and he needed to make money. As he recounted to me, he started producing Mission-style furniture, and the pieces sold. Then someone offered him a vacant house in which to display his furniture, and the house, which had been on the market for months, quickly sold. He furnished another house that was for sale, which was also snapped up, and then started building his own. Within four or five years, Cliff had built more than thirty houses in and around San Diego. And then he came to Los Angeles.

In Cliff's early days as an architect, his style looked a lot like nineteenth-century Californian; he called one of his houses a "haciendita," which gives you some idea of his traditionalist background.

His great motto was "The plan is shaped by the materials." His most famous work is probably the Roper house, which he designed on speculation in 1933, a fairly modest place that showcased his basic architectural ideas and a muted color scheme. Cliff had a formula that stayed the same no matter the fundamental style of the house:

1. Fit the house to the site; the facade the public sees is often fairly bland.
2. Use natural materials (plaster, hand-worked beams, roof tiles, terra-cotta pavers).
3. The patio—or courtyard—is key.

The overall effect was gracious and relaxed. Cliff's houses were built to be enjoyed; with their wide verandas and muted color schemes, they felt comfortable. The breakfast room was always oriented toward the rising sun, the living room for southern exposure.

Cliff designed to the market; it wasn't unusual for him to simultaneously work on several different houses in completely different styles. In the 1950s he designed several hundred tract houses in Long Beach that, while ranch houses, derived from the International Style and had very little of the historic detail he loved. They were fairly inexpensive, and they relied on open floor plans with a lot of light and private courtyards.

In the second half of his career, Cliff began getting commissions from movie stars and other wealthy clients, and he returned to his love for period details. Cliff could be completely innovative; in 1952 he designed what he called his Experimental Ranch House for his own family. The roof was primarily fabric and was made to roll up; most of the interior walls were on rubber wheels, so the spaces could be reconfigured at will.

Mary E. Nichols / *Architectural Digest* May 1987

Yours truly with my elegant and talented friend Cliff May.

Our bedroom on Old Oak Road.

Mary E. Nichols / *Architectural Digest* May 1987

Mary E. Nichols / *Architectural Digest* May 1987

The signature Cliff May bird tower at our house. He gave us six pairs of Slow Roller pigeons that gave us so much pleasure.

I was honored to buy a house that Cliff had designed for his own family. Architectural historians refer to it as Cliff May House #3, which was built in the late 1930s on Old Oak Road, right off Sunset Boulevard. Cliff and his family lived there for fourteen years; then, in 1949, he added another 3,200 square feet, very nearly doubling the size. After I bought it in 1982, Cliff remodeled it yet again for our family.

It's a low, rambling house, a brilliant solution for fitting a horse ranch into what was a suburban lot. It had a shake roof and a stable on the property for the horses that he, my wife Jill, my daughter Natasha, and I loved to ride. Originally it had three bedrooms, a maid's room, three patios, a stable, a tack room, and a paddock. Over the years both the house and the horse areas were enlarged. The remodels made it one of Cliff's California ramblers; it ended up designed like a wagon wheel, with the central living space in the center and several corridors leading out from there to the bedrooms and offices.

In 1947, Elizabeth Gordon of *House Beautiful* called Cliff's #3 "the most significant ranch house in America," an honor I had no concept of when I bought the place. I just thought it was an ideal place to raise my kids after a terrible tragedy, and I was proved right.

We rode horses there; we had countless meals there; we healed there. Jill and I were married there; my daughters, Natasha and Kate, and my son, Peter Donen, were all married there. It holds a special place in all our memories and always will.

It was less than a mile off Sunset Boulevard, but it felt as if you were a million miles away from the hurly-burly of Hollywood. I lived in Cliff May House #3 very happily for twenty-five years. Cliff once told me that people who don't live in ranch houses "don't know how to live."

*

There was an interesting way of determining social standing in the parties of that era. Contrary to cynical popular belief, if your box office popularity fell off, you weren't suddenly dropped from A-list parties; once you were in the group, you were in the group. If you were coming off a long list of flops, you might not be seated at the A table, but you'd still be in the A group. In that respect, I don't think the movie business is really much different from any other business.

The great hostesses of Hollywood were more domestic entrepreneurs than they were chefs. Very few of them would spend much time in the kitchen; most contented themselves with planning and executing their soirees, or perhaps making a special hors d'oeuvre that they knew they could do well.

But there were a few exceptions. Connie Wald, Jerry Wald's wife, did most of the cooking for her parties herself, and Jerry took a lot of pride in his wife's abilities in the kitchen. Jerry, of course, was a huge promoter, and had a great ability to put the pieces of projects together.

Jerry didn't make great pictures, but rather commercial ones that were solid entertainment. He was supposedly Budd Schulberg's inspiration for *What Makes Sammy Run?*, although that implies a guy with more hustle than talent, and I always found Jerry to be a genuine hands-on producer. Connie, who was always at his side, lived to a very ripe old age, and when she died in 2012 she left instructions that she didn't want a funeral; instead, all the people who loved her were to have a great dinner—at Connie's expense.

Another couple who were among the greatest party givers of

that period were Bill and Edie Goetz. After World War II, as a young producer Bill Goetz started a production company called International Pictures. A few years later, he merged International with Universal and became a wealthy man.

From the outside there was nothing special about the Goetzes' house. It was two stories, was painted a light gray, and had a wrought-iron porte cochere—just another house in Holmby Hills with interiors by William Haines, one of dozens in the neighborhood.

It was only when you stepped inside the house that you realized you were someplace special, for the walls were covered with the most spectacular display of Impressionist art outside the Musée d'Orsay. Bill and Edie had one of the finest private art collections in America. That was why Edie always entertained at home—it gave guests a chance to appreciate the collection, and it gave her a chance to show it off. Bill and Edie's attitude toward their extraordinary assemblage of art was low key. They weren't so presumptuous as to offer a guided tour, but if you had half a brain you'd ask them about some of the paintings—and how they'd gotten their hands on them. They wanted to share their objects of beauty with people.

The living room alone featured Cézanne's *La Maison du Pendu*, Bonnard's *Portrait of a Young Woman*, Manet's *Woman with Umbrella*, Renoir's *Nature Morte, Fleurs et Fruits* and Picasso's *Maternité*. A Degas bronze ballerina sat on a table. I remember touching its skirt with awe, and hoping nobody noticed me.

In the sitting room over the fireplace was Van Gogh's *Étude à la Bougie*, and the dining room contained a Sheraton table and Georgian silver. The walls featured Degas's *Two Dancers in Repose* and a Bonnard called *Le Dejeuner*. Another wall featured a Monet, a

Courtesy of Victoria Shepherd—Bleeden

William Goetz seated with a portion of his art collection.

Sisley, and, if I remember correctly, a Toulouse-Lautrec, which were all mounted on a wall that rose to reveal the projection room that was a standard feature for producers of Bill's stature.

It was the screening room that drove people up the wall—to raise a Monet to watch a crappy movie, or even a good movie, struck some as the height of nouveau riche behavior. Irene Mayer Selznick, Edie's sister, would tell everyone what poor taste she thought it reflected, even though the art itself was beyond reproach—well bought, and well displayed.

Edie and Irene were the daughters of Louis B. Mayer and they never really got along, mostly because they were extremely competitive. Each of them married an aspiring producer—Irene to David Selznick, Edie to Bill Goetz. David achieved greatness, Bill achieved success. There was, needless to say, a great deal of tsuris in the family, of jostling and unease.

Irene would eventually divorce David over his affair with Jennifer Jones, while Edie and Bill stayed married—quite happily, I believe. I met Irene only once or twice, just long enough to sense how very different the sisters were. To put it in a nutshell, Irene was intellectual and Edie was social. Each of them understood the movie business backward and forward, although in different ways—Irene creatively, Edie in terms of politics and power.

I found Edie to be a very open person—if she liked you. If she didn't, she simply didn't bother with you. But it would be unfair to call her a snob; I always found her to be a gracious and generous woman, in attitude as well as spirit.

Frankly, with the art the Goetzes owned, the food and the company could have been drawn from Skid Row and it wouldn't have diminished my appreciation. But Edie and Bill were strictly A-list—their guests were the Gary Coopers, the Jimmy Stewarts. Edie's invitation would tell you whether the event was black tie or just to wear a business suit. The atmosphere was formal but not stiff. That is to say, if you knew Edie and the other guests, you'd be fine. If you didn't, I imagine it would have been intimidating.

Edie's staff was up to the standards of her guests. She always let it be known that her butler had once buttled for the Queen Mum at Buckingham Palace. Edie always had the finest of everything—food, wines, crystal, china.

Edie Goetz was *the* hostess of her generation—her only true competition was Rocky Cooper, Gary's wife—and the women who came to Edie's parties knew it. The women would trot out their best clothes, predominantly from couturiers. I remember a lot of Jimmy Galanos dresses, and I remember a lot of stunning jewelry—the real thing, not replicas.

Edie and Bill's house was no place for false fronts. The paintings were real, the success of the guests was real, and so were the accoutrements of that success. The women wore their finest because they were part of an evening of special people, and they were proud to show off their best. (In line with that, drinking was rarely a problem at A-list parties of this period. People were expected to know their limits and behave accordingly, and if they didn't, they would very quietly be steered in a different direction or, in extreme cases, steered home. Unseemly behavior was rare.)

Bill Goetz was a funny, jolly man, with a deep, throaty voice like Ben Gazzara's. He was a Democrat, although politics wasn't what drove the wedge between him and his ardently Republican father-in-law. In 1952 Bill cosponsored a fund-raiser for Adlai Stevenson with Dore Schary, who had deposed Louis B. Mayer from MGM, the studio he had founded and that carried his name. Mayer begged his daughter to intervene and prevent what he felt to be further crushing humiliation at Schary's hands, but she felt she had to remain loyal to her husband.

Mayer never forgave either of them. By the time he died five years later, he'd cut Edie and her children out of his will.

After that, the temperature between Irene and Edie never got much above freezing; it was the divided halves of the Warner family all over again. These men could forge empires, but the forging of functional families did not seem to be in their skill sets.

Bill Goetz died in 1969, and Edie hung on for nearly twenty years after that, although the parties gradually dried up. When Edie died in 1988, most of her estate consisted of the art collection on the walls. It was auctioned off for eighty million dollars—more than the estates of her father and sister combined.

Today, just one of those paintings would bring eighty million dollars, or close to it. I shudder to think what the entire collection would bring, not that anybody but a Silicon Valley entrepreneur could afford it. Today the major art collections in Hollywood tend toward the modern, filled with still living or recently dead artists whose work costs much less. Amassing a collection like that is more of a gamble, and I would wager it's not as much fun.

That's the way Bill and Edie Goetz would have looked at it.

Very few stars' houses were as grand as the Goetzes'. Jimmy and Gloria Stewart's Tudor-style house on Roxbury Drive in Beverly Hills was quite homey and unpretentious. Jimmy did what I thought was a very classy, not to mention telling, thing: he bought the house next door, tore it down, and planted a garden. He and Gloria would be out there all the time, supervising the gardeners or harvesting flowers and vegetables.

Inside the house, the piano in the living room was covered with pictures of family and friends, only some of whom were famous. Other than that, it was a comfortable home, with splashes of orange in the furnishings, but otherwise unremarkable. It could have been the home of a banker in Chagrin Falls.

The only room that told you who owned the house was the library. There was a niche that held Jimmy's Oscar, as well as his certificate from the New York Film Critics Circle for Best Actor of 1939 for *Mr. Smith Goes to Washington*. There was a citation from the air force—Jimmy flew many combat missions during World War II—and lots of photos. Oh, and one other thing—there was a small statue of a rabbit in there as well: Elwood P. Dowd's old friend Harvey.

Some of the photos were stills from movies, although interestingly they weren't necessarily shots from films regarded as classics—there was nothing from *Rear Window* or *Mr. Smith*, for instance. Instead, Jimmy featured shots from *Winchester '73*, *The Stratton Story*, and *The Glenn Miller Story*. The others were simply family photos: Jimmy's beloved twin girls; Jimmy's father's hardware store in Indiana, Pennsylvania; Jimmy visiting Vietnam. In that sense, the house was a true reflection of the man Jimmy was: a family man who was as much a product of Pennsylvania as of Hollywood.

Toward the end of his life, Jimmy and I were shooting a promotional film for St. John's Hospital, the charity to which Jimmy devoted so much time and energy. After we finished the scene, we were walking away from the camera crew when an old wino staggered down the street and saw who was coming toward him.

"Hey, Jimmy," he said. "Where's Harvey?"

And without missing a beat, Jimmy, with his inimitable stutter, said, "Why, H-H-Harvey's *everywhere!*"

In his will, Jimmy named me to replace him as a director of St. John's, and I've continued on the board down to the present day. It's the least I can do to show my love and gratitude to such a great actor, such a superb human being.

When people think of beautiful Hollywood women, they think of movie stars, but there were extravagantly lovely women who were not actresses. Billy Wilder's wife Audrey, for instance, was one of the chicest women I've ever seen in my life.

When I knew them, Billy and Audrey had an apartment on Wilshire that was overflowing with his splendid modern art collection—Schiele, Klee, Braque, Miró, Balthus, Picasso—all the artists that Billy had admired when they, and he, were starting out in Europe but that he didn't have the money to buy until he became successful in Hollywood. There were also a couple of comparative latecomers to Billy's collection—Saul Steinberg and David Hockney—but they were friends, so they were in on a pass.

A few years before he died, Billy decided to sell off some of his art, and made more than thirty million dollars at auction—more than he'd ever made in the movie business. Not only that, but Billy said that the art was a lot more fun than the movie business, which is always like pushing a huge boulder uphill.

The Wilders' apartment wasn't really big enough to entertain more than a handful of people, so most of Billy's parties took place at Chasen's or at L'Escoffier at the Beverly Hilton. When Billy and Audrey threw a party, it was a particularly delicious affair, because their level of taste and style was so high. These affairs were strictly black tie, and they tended to be centered on Billy's or Audrey's birthdays or their wedding anniversary. There would be a small orchestra, and the guest list always included Jack Lemmon and his wife, Felicia Farr.

Billy was an adorable man, a combination of the acerbity of Berlin, where he worked as a newspaper reporter in the Weimar era, and of the far more benevolent Vienna—he was born in Austria. If you asked him, he would talk about his old pictures, but you had to ask him. When he did discuss them, it was with a remarkable level of objectivity, probably because he wasn't the sort of man who dwelled in the past.

Billy didn't go through his long life wondering about why one picture was a hit and another picture was a flop. Maybe he should have used Cary Grant instead of Gary Cooper, maybe the problem was the script, maybe the problem was the director (both jobs often filled by Wilder himself). He would shrug his shoulders and say, "The hell with it!"—about success or failure alike. Although, like anybody else, he found the successes lots more fun and a lot more lucrative.

Billy had copies of his scripts, but he didn't read them, and he didn't have 16mm or 35mm prints of his films. If they were shown on TV, he didn't watch them, and he evinced only polite interest if you watched them and wanted to talk about them.

He once explained to me why he was able to maintain an emotional distance about his movies. It involved one of the pictures he made in the 1960s. He had assembled his first choice in every area—I. A. L. Diamond had written the script with Billy, and Billy had gotten his first choice of cameraman and composer. The cast was just what Billy wanted.

After having spent nearly two years of his life working on the film, it was finally ready to be shown to the public for the first time. The preview was in Westwood, and Billy was understandably nervous. Anxious to get firsthand reactions, he hovered in the lobby as the show was breaking, and fell in step behind a young couple who were leaving the theater.

"What did you think?" asked the young woman.

The young man sighed and said, "Where do you want to have dinner?"

For Billy, that was an eye-opener. He'd had great successes and great failures, and he would always insist that he had worked just as hard on the failures as he had on the successes—*The Spirit of St. Louis* was one of the biggest financial disasters in the history of Warner Bros. Why some pictures soared from their first day while others sputtered, strained, and dropped was one of the mysteries of the universe, and Billy didn't pretend to understand it.

All that work . . . And as far as the audience was concerned, it was just a diversion, something to fill the time before dinner.

I think Billy was always subtly embarrassed by critics theorizing about him, whether for or against, because so much of what he did—what any creative person does—derived from a passion for the material. And how do you analyze passion? You feel it or you don't. Billy didn't like being ignored, but he didn't like being taken too seriously, either.

Like so many of the truly creative people in Hollywood, Billy was focused on the next movie, not the last one, so his enforced retirement must have been very tough on him. Not that he ever let on—he didn't want sympathy. He knew his career had been close to unparalleled, and he wasn't given to self-pity.

After Billy died, Audrey carried on, through years of declining health, until her death in 2012. Because Billy was a famous filmmaker, the world knew how special he was—not just as an artist, but as a man. But a man like Billy had to have a special woman, and Audrey was truly that.

Someone once asked my wife Jill why she thought Billy and Audrey's marriage had worked.

"Because they loved each other," she said.

And that says it all.

By the 1950s, tastes had definitively changed, and the vast Spanish and Italianate mansions seemed permanently passé. They were also incredibly expensive to run, so it became cheaper to tear them down, as was the case with Marion Davies's great beach house at Santa Monica. The destruction of the great mansions sped up over the succeeding years. Even Pickfair, the original movie mansion, was leveled in 1990.

The years of the great parties were beginning to fade as well. There were many reasons for that. I had usually hung out with a crowd that was ten to fifteen years older than I was, so as those people aged they had less to celebrate. Some died, and some just left

Hollywood, so the nucleus got smaller and smaller. And the business got more diversified. TV people worked much more and longer hours than movie people, so they tended to go to bed earlier. Finally, the great restaurants that had hosted so many great parties began going out of business.

It was a classic generational shift.

It was a lesson to me that nothing lasts forever. Except the movies.

Playtime

From its inception, the movie business attracted extremely ambitious, type A personalities for whom the making of motion pictures was an all-consuming activity. This meant that blowing off steam in between films or on weekends became even more important than it would have ordinarily been.

People who were working in the industry in the early days told me that a lot of the pastimes enjoyed by the stars were on the innocent side. Besides fads like theme parties, there were also all sorts of games that ran through groups like wildfire, mostly variations on charades.

Carole Lombard once threw a party on a hospital theme, with equipment rented from a medical supply company. Each guest was given a hospital gown to wear over his or her evening clothes and was then led to a standard-issue hospital bed. Dinner was served at an operating table.

Lombard's most epic party probably came in 1935, when she took over the entire Ocean Park amusement pier and invited a couple of hundred friends to come in street clothes. There were stars there, of course—Cary Grant, Marlene Dietrich, Errol Flynn—but there were also the grips and extras and crew members that she valued just as highly as the members of her peer group.

The influence that stars had in that era seems remarkable today, simply because there was no real competition for the public's attention. Back then, there were movies and, to a much lesser extent, radio. That was it.

Everybody has heard the story of how Clark Gable's lack of an undershirt in *It Happened One Night* devastated undershirt sales all across the country. But the desire to emulate the stars went deeper than just clothes. A few years before that, when Norma and Constance Talmadge opened up a subdivision of ranch and Mission-style houses in San Diego, contractors across the country got requests for duplicates. The subdivision was called Talmadge, and the designer was Cliff May.

The 1920s soirees thrown by Douglas Fairbanks and Mary Pickford were far from the wildest, but they assuredly had the highest percentage of royal guests. That was partly because Fairbanks was a devout Anglophile, and partly because inherited royalty is always curious to meet other varieties. The fact that American royalty is earned and the other variety is inherited probably doesn't matter. Whatever the circumstances of their position, the rich have problems that only the rich can understand.

One typical party was a formal dinner dance at Pickfair thrown for Prince George, son of George V of England. The guest list included Mary Astor, Charlie Chaplin, Ronald Colman, Lili Damita, Greta Garbo, John Gilbert, Jetta Goudal, John Loder, Bessie Love, Tom Mix, Ramon Novarro, Norma Shearer, Irving Thalberg, Lupe Vélez, and Gloria Swanson.

It's an impressive roster. What's even more impressive is that Mary Pickford pulled the party together with precisely one day's notice.

During dinner, Prince George told Gloria Swanson that he hoped to see more than just Pickfair during his brief time in Hollywood. Swanson needed to hear no more; she called home and instructed her butler to deliver champagne to her Rolls, which was parked outside Pickfair. As the party began to wind down, Swanson and the prince, along with a couple of others, headed for a nightclub in Culver City.

After the nightclub closed at three in the morning, they headed back to Swanson's house, dragging the orchestra from the nightclub with them. Eventually breakfast was served, and Charlie Chaplin kept everybody entertained by doing his party

Douglas Fairbanks, Mary Pickford, and Charlie Chaplin at Pickfair for a New Year's party.

Everett Collection

routines—impersonations and set pieces he had honed over the years, all reputedly hilarious. Eventually, they got the prince back to the train station.

Now *that's* a party!

When I came to Hollywood, the most prodigious party givers were Basil and Ouida Rathbone, both ferociously social. For their eleventh wedding anniversary, they invited 250 people to the restaurant Victor Hugo, which had been converted into a cathedral by dint of papier-mâché. The theme of the evening was "famous couples." Rathbone and his wife were dressed as the Emperor Franz Joseph and the Empress of Austria; Eddie Robinson and his wife came as Napoléon and Joséphine; Jeanette MacDonald and Gene Raymond came as Romeo and Juliet.

Rathbone was a hardworking character actor and a multifaceted

Jack Warner with Edward G. Robinson and his wife, Gladys Lloyd, at Basil and Ouida Rathbone's eleventh wedding anniversary at Victor Hugo's restaurant.

individual, which many actors are not. He'd been decorated for his service in World War I, was an expert fencer—there was a reason he made a lot of swashbucklers—and as an actor he was capable of giving a character a lot of different colors. He made a great deal of money throughout the 1930s and especially in the 1940s, playing Sherlock Holmes in a long-running radio series as well as a batch of films at Fox and Universal. But when he died in 1967, he left an estate of only ten thousand dollars.

Parties are expensive, but I'll bet he had a ball.

Hollywood parties often featured some great practical jokes and running gags. There was a mousy character actor named Vince Barnett who became locally famous for moonlighting as a practical joker, generally under the guise of an insulting waiter. I saw Barnett in action, and he was hysterical. At one party, he would accuse the guests of stealing the silver; at another, he would yell at Charlie Chaplin for hogging attention. When he was introduced to Helen Hayes, he told her he could feel only pity for anyone married to a rat bastard like Charles MacArthur.

Barnett could be brutal, a lot like Don Rickles in the modern era. Both men played to an element of self-loathing in show business—many successful people feel like fakers who are just getting by, and there's nothing more terrifying than the possibility of being caught . . . or funnier than being called on it by someone who knows how to do it.

By the late 1930s the Hollywood social networks were already largely worked out. The Germans tended to hang out at Ernst Lubitsch's house in Beverly Hills when they weren't at Salka Viertel's in the Palisades. Literary types were often found at Edmund Goulding's or George Cukor's. The very old guard that used to hang around at Pickfair had broken up when Douglas Fairbanks and Mary Pickford divorced, but there was an elite group that was still invited to Charlie Chaplin's house on Summit Drive for Sunday tennis, where he served tea from a large silver pot along with English sandwiches with the crusts cut off.

Louis B. Mayer had a Sunday open house at his place on the Santa Monica beach. It had been designed by MGM's art director Cedric Gibbons in a Spanish style, and the walls were a foot thick for insulation against the heat of the summer. Mayer's place was no cottage; it had twenty rooms and onyx and marble bathrooms installed by artisans imported from Greece.

The director James Cruze also had regular open houses at his Flintridge estate in the years before his death in 1942. He offered a large table piled with ham and roast beef sandwiches, and there was also a jardiniere just inside his front door filled with change, so that anyone who was financially inconvenienced could take a few dollars to get through the week.

Recreation around Hollywood wasn't radically different from recreation anyplace else. There was golf—the best golfer of his generation was probably Bing Crosby, who had a handicap of precisely two.

I've come to believe that golf has been nearly as important to me as acting. If I had to characterize what the game has given me, I'd say a sense of manners, to go along with an abiding sense of humility, if only because golf is a game that *will* kick your ass. It teaches you how to deal with failure. In golf, sometimes things work and sometimes they don't—just like in life. The game is fundamentally impossible—you will never conquer it, but it has a way of teasing you by giving you just enough success to keep you playing.

Golf has also opened up a lot of great, enduring friendships. And it's a game you can take with you anywhere and practice all your life, as I proved when I shot my age at eighty-two.

Not that I'm bragging.

There was a period of a couple of months when I was a scratch golfer, but that was because all I was doing was hitting balls instead of reading scripts. For most of my life, I've played to an eight or ten handicap.

I come by my passion for the sport naturally; my father was a member at Bel Air Country Club practically from the time we moved there. When I was twenty-one, I paid the transfer fee to become a member myself. I would give up that membership when I went to Europe in the early 1960s, and there were a few other periods when I couldn't play much—when my daughter Katie was born, and when Natalie and I married the second time and we had Natasha and Courtney to take care of. But about fifteen years ago I bought Howard Keel's membership at Bel Air, and the circle closed. Now I'm a senior member and proud of it.

In the 1950s, and in the 1980s and 1990s and since, when I con-sciously took my foot off the gas pedal of my career, I played all the time, all over town and all over the world. I've played at Troon and St. Andrews in Scotland, and I shot a seventy-seven at Prestwich. I've had three hole-in-ones—at Bel Air, at Cypress Point, and at the Los Angeles Country Club.

Not that I'm bragging.

One of my proudest moments in golf came when I beat Sam Snead on *Shell's Wonderful World of Golf.* It was a TV program in which Snead would take on various golf-mad celebrities, who got to play with their handicaps.

I knew Snead and had seen him at Bel Air several times. Sam

liked to drink, and he was not averse to randomly chosen female companionship. I figured that if I got him early in the morning for a game, before the fog of the previous evening had cleared, I might have a chance.

The round was magical—I was all over him. It came down to the last hole. I had to make an eighteen-inch putt to win, because he wouldn't give it to me. My hands were shaking, but I made the putt. I didn't beat him straight up, but I beat him. And then Snead wouldn't shake my hand. The program gave me a trophy, and I've still got it.

Fully twenty-five years later, in Palm Springs, there was Sam again. I went over to say hi.

Me playing a round of golf, circa 1955.

"You son of a bitch," he said.

He was a terrible loser, but that's probably why he was Sam Snead.

I've played with Jack Nicklaus and Arnold Palmer and Gary Player. I've played with Bing Crosby—great swing, and a passion for the game—and I've played at all the clubs around Los Angeles. At Lakeside, I played mostly with Don Johnson, Howard Keel, and Bob Hope.

At Hillcrest, I was even asked to become a member, which was an honor because Hillcrest is the Jewish country club. I love Hillcrest, for the company as well as for the course and for the food. Hillcrest has always had the best food of any country club I've played at. Groucho, Zeppo, and even Chico Marx were there all the time, as was George Burns. No, they didn't golf—my usual golf partners at Hillside were Abe Lastfogel, Bud Yorkin, or Danny Kaye—but they kibitzed in the restaurant and the card room.

Of all the courses I've played, the most memorable was Augusta. To walk that land, to walk over that bridge, following in the footsteps of the great men who have become legends there, was a great honor.

But if someone were to tell me I could play only one more round of golf, it wouldn't be at Augusta, but at Bel Air. I caddied there as a boy, saw Fred Astaire and Cary Grant and Randolph Scott and Clark Gable play there, and even had the temerity to offer Gable some advice about his putting, which turned out to be helpful.

Fred Astaire and I played at Bel Air often, usually nine holes very early in the morning. Actors don't practice that much, and Fred was no exception—his handicap was in the teens—but as you might expect he had a beautifully rhythmic swing. (There are some actors who practice a great deal; Dennis Quaid and Jack Wagner are scratch golfers, or close to it.)

These days, I usually play Bel Air with Mike Connors, Grant Tinker, and Steven Goldberg. I love the course, and I know it so well—each blade of grass is familiar. Maybe I love it so much *because* I know it so well. With golf, familiarity doesn't breed contempt, but satisfaction and tranquility.

Unless you shank an iron or blow an eighteen-inch putt. Then it produces rage. A fair trade-off for all the great times I've had on the golf courses of the world.

In the early 1990s, the producer David Wolper was making a film in collaboration with the USGA. We took the Warner Bros. corporate plane and traveled around the country, making sure to play every great course in America while shooting the documentary. To this day, I'm not sure which was the sideline—the golf we played or the documentary. Either way, it was one of the most pleasurable perks I've had in what I have to consider, on balance, a very lucky life.

Those people who didn't golf often had boats—some of the most beautiful yachts were owned by the best and richest directors. I'm thinking of John Ford's *Araner* and Cecil B. DeMille's *Seaward*, both very impressive yachts. But even people who were much lower on the totem pole were serious sailors, like the character actor Frank Morgan, who kept scrapbooks about his yachting victories, which I believe included winning the Los Angeles to Honolulu race. Morgan loved to drink and sometimes did it at the Bel Air Country Club, where he was a member and where I knew him to say hello to. Other quality sailors were Errol Flynn (*Zaca*) and Humphrey Bogart (*Santana*).

Charlie Chaplin had a much smaller boat, *Panacea*, but it didn't

Errol Flynn heading for the crow's nest on his gorgeous yacht, *Zaca*.

get an awful lot of use because Chaplin's preferred recreation involved playing tennis on the court at his house.

Out in Santa Monica were the Santa Monica Swimming Club and the Santa Monica Beach Club, whose members competed against each other in fierce volleyball games, seven men on a team. Joel McCrea and George O'Brien played for one team, Buster Crabbe for another. Cary Grant was around there at the time, too, working on the tan he always had.

Other people were interested in more earthbound hobbies. Racing, for instance. The comedy producer Hal Roach came up with the idea of the Santa Anita track, and Bing Crosby was president of Del Mar, near San Diego. Hollywood Park was organized by Jack Warner, who was chairman of the board, along with Raoul Walsh.

Hollywood Park became such an entertainment mainstay for the studios that both *Variety* and the *Hollywood Reporter* would print racing charts and results. If tourists were smart, they would usually head either to the racetracks or to the American Legion stadium in Hollywood, because they'd be sure to find a dozen or so stars there to snag for an autograph.

People with money to spend naturally look for ways to spend it, and horses are among the quickest ways to disperse a fortune. Harry and Jack Warner both had stables, as did Louis B. Mayer, whose stable was one of the top half dozen in the country for a number of years. It was Mayer who raised the standards of California stables to the point where they nearly achieved equality with their great counterparts in Kentucky. Others who had stables included Bing Crosby, Errol Flynn, Don Ameche, Myron Selznick, and William Goetz. Barbara Stanwyck and Zeppo Marx were partners in a stable called Marwyck.

Fred Astaire just loved the horses, and he owned a string of thoroughbreds that included a horse named Triplicate. Fred paid six thousand dollars for Triplicate and the horse went on to win over a quarter million dollars.

Walt Disney was a great polo enthusiast for a number of years, as were Spencer Tracy (a reckless player), Darryl Zanuck, Robert Montgomery, Gary Cooper, Hal Roach, Jack Holt, Leo Carrillo, and Charlie Farrell.

Polo necessitated owning a string of horses and having a total lack of fear of falling. The best of the polo players was probably Will Rogers, simply because he had the most experience with horses. Today Rogers's polo field is part of Will Rogers State Park.

Darryl Zanuck at Howard Hawks's East-West croquet match in Beverly Hills in 1946.

For years I rode my own horses around the periphery of the field where Rogers and Darryl used to bang their horses and their heads.

Darryl was a very tough polo player, with a large stable of ponies, but when I went to work for him after the war, he became more involved with croquet, which made the Fox stockholders much happier.

Croquet was the postwar sport du jour for the upper echelon in Hollywood, whose particular nature as an enclave became apparent with the enthusiasm for such a genteel sport, which up to then had been confined to places like Palm Beach or Newport. Also contributing to its fashionable aspect were requirements that held a certain snob appeal, for very few people could qualify—you needed a very wide, perfectly flat, expertly manicured grass field cut to the length of a putting green.

Croquet is reasonably entertaining to play, even though it takes forever to complete a game—a competition can go on all day and into the night, so you need a lot of stamina. At its most competitive, it's not unlike playing thirty-six holes of golf.

My only problem with croquet is that it's deadly dull to watch. I think its appeal was primarily to a group of people who were getting a little old for the hell-bent-for-leather aspects of polo but had to have something equally competitive—and croquet can be utterly vicious.

The first impetus for croquet had come from the East Coast in the 1920s, with the Algonquin Round Table crowd. Herbert Bayard Swope and Alexander Woollcott had croquet courts, and other people who played included Averell Harriman, Harpo Marx, Richard Rodgers, and Vincent Astor. I seem to recall that it was Moss Hart who brought the sport to the West Coast during World War II and introduced it to Darryl Zanuck, who regarded him very highly as a writer. Soon Zanuck introduced the game to all of his friends: Howard Hawks and Hawks's brother Bill, Sam Goldwyn, Gregory Ratoff.

Croquet courts suddenly began appearing all over Beverly Hills, and Zanuck and Goldwyn would play for as much as a thousand dollars a game. Goldwyn was something of a fanatic about physical fitness, which may be why he lived into his nineties. His natural enthusiasms were for long walks and handball, but the latter became difficult after he broke an ankle. His second love, golf, simply made him too upset—one bad shot would lead to four more, which would lead to a ruined afternoon and, as the man said, a good walk spoiled.

Harpo Marx and Alexander Woollcott introduced Goldwyn to croquet, and his wife Frances built a court for him. The simple house rules were printed on a blackboard by a scorekeeper's hut, which was actually a bar:

1. Don't get excited.
2. Correctly remember balls you are dead on.
3. Have patience with fellow members who are not as good as you are.

Croquet is usually a sedate sport, although nothing was sedate when Sam Goldwyn played it. It was his court, so he felt entitled to ignore his own rules when he felt like it.

The addicts, the people who were always at either Darryl's court in Palm Springs or at Sam's court in LA, were Louis Jourdan—who I believe was the best player of them all—Joe Cotten, Clifton Webb, Ty Power, and Cesar Romero. If the game was in Palm Springs, William Powell would act as the official cheerleader.

The high point of the craze for croquet was probably in July 1946, when Howard Hawks hosted a best-of-three East-West croquet championship. Moss Hart, Ty Power, and agent Felix Ferry played for the East, against Darryl and Hawks for the West. Floodlights were installed so the matches could go on far into the night. Zanuck and Hawks won the first game, but I was told that they got overconfident and proceeded to lose the second and third games, giving the victory to the East.

For the rest of us who went to Darryl's Santa Monica house, there were other games. I recall marathon poker sessions among a round-robin that included Robert Capa, Constance Bennett, Lew Wasserman, and Howard Hawks's wife Slim Keith. Sometimes, if

Restaurateur Mike Romanoff, right, playing croquet with film producer Samuel Goldwyn.

Darryl wasn't in the mood for poker or croquet, he'd play board games such as Labyrinth.

Others enjoyed hunting and fishing; Clark Gable and Robert Taylor were among this crowd. Gable particularly enjoyed the Teal, a club south of Bakersfield where I was also a member, or the La Grulla Gun Club in the Baja Mountains near Ensenada. For fishing, Clark would head to the Rogue River in Oregon.

A much smaller subset enjoyed flying, but that was nearly as expensive as sailing. Ben Lyon and Bebe Daniels were among the first stars to pilot their own planes; others included Ray Milland, Wallace Beery, George Brent, and Jimmy Stewart, who, as I've mentioned, was a superb pilot from his missions in World War II. Robert Taylor also flew his own plane, and there were some successful directors who flew as well, among them Henry King and Clarence Brown. As a matter of fact, Brown would fly his plane to work—he'd land at the Culver City airport, take a car to MGM, and at the end of the day fly back home.

Nice work if you can get it.

Style

have long maintained that the most influential figure in twentieth-century American fashion was an Englishman: the Duke of Windsor. I realize that posterity has not dealt kindly with the duke—there was that flirtation with the Nazis during World War II, and succeeding decades spent drifting around the world without purpose.

But when it came to matters of style, Edward obliterated the expectation of rigid conformity that was the norm when he was a boy.

In the years when he was the heir to the throne, he was by far the world's most eligible bachelor, and everything he wore was immediately copied. He avoided stiff evening clothes, preferring midnight blue tuxedos. He wore double-breasted suits, often in a gray chalk stripe. He also liked Fair Isle sweaters, and anything with a check pattern immediately became part of every Englishman's—and a good many Americans'—wardrobe.

The duke's first acolyte wasn't an Englishman, and he wasn't an American, either. He was Italian: Rudolph Valentino is recorded in the ledgers of bespoke tailors like Huntsman in 1923 and Anderson & Sheppard in 1924. Valentino's relationship with his tailors was cut short as he died young, but the allegiance to a Savile Row tailor often transcended generations, and even sexes.

Marlene Dietrich was introduced to Anderson & Sheppard by Douglas Fairbanks Jr. in 1936, when they were having an affair. Fairbanks had been infused with enthusiasm for Savile Row by his father. Dietrich's relationship with Fairbanks didn't last, but she stayed with Anderson & Sheppard for decades—they tailored all the flannels, tweeds, and blazers that she wore off-screen.

It's interesting to note that while the wardrobes of actresses were all rigorously controlled by the studios, the wardrobes of the actors were largely left up to their own taste. Nobody got near Marlene Dietrich's movie wardrobe but Travis Banton and Josef von Sternberg. Her leading men, however—Gary Cooper, Cary Grant, Charles Boyer, Robert Donat—were all regularly outfitted on Savile Row. When I knew him in the 1950s, Gary dressed mostly in Brooks Brothers. Cary Grant wore Kilgour, French & Stanbury, who made the gray suit he wore in *North by Northwest*. It never got wrinkled. But then, neither did Cary.

There were two men who were at the leading edge of the British cut in Hollywood: Douglas Fairbanks Sr. and Fred Astaire. Both of them had lower-middle-class upbringings—Fred from Nebraska, Fairbanks from Colorado. More important, both were fairly devout Anglophiles, perhaps because it was another way of leaving the hometown and the rough early years behind.

Fred once recalled his first meeting with the Prince of Wales in 1924, when he was working in London with his beloved sister Adele in Gershwin's *Stop Flirting*. Edward, he said, "was unquestionably the best-dressed young man in the world. I was missing none of it. I noted particularly the white waistcoat did not show below the dress-coat front. I liked that."

Fred made some inquiries but found that the prince's tailor—
Hawes & Curtis—would not work for him because he was a mere
actor. But Anderson & Sheppard would.

Fred was immediately won over: "It was difficult not to order
one of every cloth that was shown to me, particularly the vicuña."
(Fred loved Anderson & Sheppard, but the tuxedo he wore in 1935's
Top Hat was tailored by Kilgour, French & Stanbury.)

Fred took the prince's look and brought his own creativity to it.
Buying stylish clothes is really more about taste than creativity, but
Fred's genius for the latter came out in his casual wardrobe. When
Fred rehearsed, he would wear gray flannels, perhaps a silk shirt,
with a scarf or a necktie knotted around his waist in homage to
Douglas Fairbanks Sr., who invented that look.

My favorite picture of the great FA

Photograph © Ellen Graham

Whether in full dress or casual, though, Fred's hands were apt to be in his pockets—he didn't like his hands. He thought they were large and ugly.

Next time you watch him dance, observe how he never has to compete with, let alone fight, his clothes—they move with him, and the soft shoulders that Anderson & Sheppard gave him glide as smoothly as Fred does. Fred's wardrobe, no matter how formal, bespoke a casual elegance that was the essence of the English cut he did so much to popularize.

In Los Angeles a tailor named Eddie Schmidt was a genius at copying anything the Savile Row firms did, but the people we're talking about were purists. Even Clark Gable, who wasn't ordinarily thought of as stunningly well dressed—probably because his body was bulkier than Fred's or Cary's—was recorded as a customer at Huntsman in 1943, as well as at Lesley & Roberts and Stovel & Mason.

By the 1950s Hollywood's taste for the English cut had moved beyond Anderson & Sheppard and Kilgour, French & Stanbury to Huntsman, who dressed actors as varied as Tyrone Power, Laurence Olivier, and Stewart Granger.

But Hollywood fashion had already begun changing radically by then. Studiously informal actors like Brando, Clift, and Dean wouldn't get dressed up for anything less than an Oscar ceremony. I understood it—I was of the same generation—but I didn't sympathize with it. My allegiance was to the styles of an earlier era.

An effective halfway house was erected by Frank Sinatra, who didn't dress English—not at all—but did attach a great deal of importance to the way he looked. His cuffs extended a half inch from his sleeves—no more and no less—and his pants ended just a tiny bit above his highly polished shoes. For a long time Frank liked his suits to be made by Sy Devore, whose clothes would be considered slightly loud today. Sy loved shine—rayons and mohairs and shark-skins. Dean Martin started buying Sy's clothes, and then Jerry Lewis did, followed by Frank and Elvis. At some point in the early sixties, Frank had 150 suits, which sounds like a lot until you remember that he owned three or four houses, with wardrobes in each, and was working incessantly.

Frank's ties were a single color, and usually silk; he liked Sulka, an enthusiasm I seem to recall he got from George Raft, who wore Sulka all the time. He also liked the ties made by Turnbull & Asser. He always had a beautifully folded handkerchief in his breast pocket—he liked to fix the handkerchief of any man who couldn't fold one as perfectly as he could, which definitely included yours truly—and he liked cuff links but not other jewelry. And let's not forget the fedora, which suited his face, but also meant that he didn't have to wear his toupee.

That's an important part of style: the way that personality makes the style work for one person in a way it wouldn't for someone with a different personality. Frank wore hats when he was a kid—and supposedly he had thirteen sport coats by the time he was in high school—but I don't honestly think he had a lasting allegiance to them. He started wearing them all the time in the early 1950s, when his hair began to thin out. That's the same reason Bing Crosby was usually seen in public with a hat. But hats looked natural on Frank, who wore snap-brims made by Cavanagh, black and gray felts, or even straw hats with pastel bands.

People who keep track of such things report that Frank wore hats on twenty of the albums he made for Capitol in the 1950s, and on another thirteen albums he made for his own company, Reprise.

And then one day Frank stopped wearing hats, sometime after men's hats went out of fashion. At the same time, he abandoned Sy

Devore, and not a moment too soon. He took up Dunhill, and Carroll & Co., which was based in Beverly Hills but made its clothes in the formal style of British tailors. When he was older, Frank went slightly informal; around the house, he would just wear a baseball cap or a golf cap.

Frank was very particular. He had rituals. He showered twice a day, sometimes more. His aftershave was witch hazel or Yardley's English Lavender. He was always adjusting his jacket, shooting his cuffs, picking an imaginary piece of lint off his coat.

Getty Images

Natalie and me with Frank Sinatra during a surprise twenty-first-birthday party held for Natalie at Romanoff's. Frank's eye is bandaged because he had been slightly injured while shooting *Never So Few* at MGM.

He was fastidious about his nails and would think nothing of using cuticle scissors or an emery board to make sure they looked good.

He loved colors—the more flamboyant the better. He liked pink, he loved orange. Around Frank, orange could be found everywhere, from his shirts to his paintings to his sweaters. As a matter of fact, the only place he would avoid orange was in a tie or a jacket.

He hated shoes that weren't polished. And if you were going out at night with Frank, you had better be wearing dark gray or black, or you'd hear about it. Frank didn't like to sit down, because it wrinkled his suits. If he had to sit down, he wouldn't cross his legs. For evening dress, Frank wouldn't wear anything but black; he didn't believe there was any excuse for wearing brown, blue, or gray after sunset.

Frank was something of a dandy, but he never gave that impression—even if he was dressed formally, his body language was relaxed, which took the edge off the formality of the clothes. Frank knew who he was, and was remarkably secure in that knowledge, which informed all of his decisions in fashion and in life.

There wasn't a lot of conversation about clothes in Hollywood beyond "Where did you get that?" But there was the occasional blazing insight. I believe that the most profound remark about Hollywood fashion—and quite possibly about Hollywood—came from Adolph Zukor, one of the founders of Paramount Pictures.

"Dress British," Zukor said, "think Yiddish."

The Press

The fan magazines wanted you to believe that stars were forever nightclubbing, moving effortlessly from their costumes into evening clothes and back again with no time left for sleeping. The movies themselves helped promote this image. We've all seen the films that Hollywood made about itself—a wide shot of the town from somewhere up in the hills, followed by a montage of the town at night, with an orgy of neon signs, usually featuring the Trocadero and the Cocoanut Grove.

Actually, nightclubbing was the norm only when you were between pictures or "on layoff." (Layoff was a brilliant invention of the studios whereby you were paid only forty weeks a year. The other twelve weeks were unpaid, and were tossed at you whenever the studio felt like it.)

If you were shooting a picture, you'd be up at five or six in the morning in order to be on the set at eight, and those days would stretch until six p.m. or later. In television, if you were doing an hour-long show every week, the hours were even longer—basically, whatever it took to get the episode finished on time.

Otherwise most of the clubbing took place on Saturdays, although there were times when the studio would want you to attend a premiere or an event on other days—even if you were working at the time—if they knew the photographers would be out in force.

For special occasions like that, a studio limo would pick you up on the set at five p.m. or so, then deposit you wherever you were to be seen. You rarely spent more than an hour at the place. The lights would go down, you'd duck out, and the limo would take you back home in order to be back on the set for your early call.

When the pictures ran, it looked as if you were a paid-up member of café society, when you'd actually been a frantic commuter, thinking only of getting home in time to memorize the next day's lines and then tumble into bed for five or six hours of sleep.

Before I began working at the studios, publicity was centered on Hedda Hopper and Louella Parsons, although there were other gossip columnists, such as Jimmy Fidler and Sheilah Graham.

It's odd how your mind associates certain people with certain events. In August 1962 I was in Montecatini, Italy, at the same time as Sheilah Graham. I was on the terrace of my hotel when she leaned out a window and yelled, "Marilyn Monroe died! Marilyn Monroe died!," to the world at large, in exactly the same way she would have announced that her building was on fire. That was how I found out that the girl I had worked with twelve years earlier, and who had since become a legend in a way nobody could have foretold, was gone.

Hedda and Louella had syndicated columns that made them very important to the industry, as did Fidler and Graham. There were also local columnists whose influence didn't extend much beyond Los Angeles but who were regarded as fairly significant. I'm thinking of Harrison Carroll at the *Los Angeles Herald-Examiner*, for instance, who really covered his beat. He was out every night, saw everybody, knew everybody, and had a way of communicating the truth without savaging people.

Beneath this group were the platoons of writers who filled up the pages of dozens of monthly fan magazines.

These publications started at just about the same time the movies did—the first one seems to have appeared in 1909. They printed copy supplied by a roster of freelancers, who numbered in the hundreds, although the bulk of their material was written by an elite group of thirty or forty writers who could produce as many as six pieces a month, some pseudonymously.

The reason they wrote so much was only partly burning ambition. Mostly, they were just trying to make a living. A writer like Adela Rogers St. John might make $125 or $150 for a lead piece, but the average fee was about half that.

The early versions of the fan magazines had periods of comparative independence, but that wasn't really in the best interests of the studios. You have to remember that, in that era, the stars were almost all under exclusive contract to one studio or another, so each studio had a vested interest in protecting its corporate assets.

After about 1934 the studios always had a publicist sit in on every interview, and most of the questions were submitted in advance. Likewise, the article itself was vetted by the studio publicity department before it was printed, to ensure that nothing indelicate found its way into print. At 20th Century Fox, there was an entire division of the publicity department that did nothing else but work with the fan magazines, and I can assure you the studio took it very seriously.

All that began to break up in the 1950s, when the studios began to divest themselves of their contract rosters as a means of saving money in the face of declining cinema attendance. Without the protection of the studio publicists, actors were forced to fend for themselves, or to rely on the independent publicists they hired, some of whom were better than others. The subsequent rise of scandal-mongering publications such as *Confidential* was a pure reaction to the decades of rigid control on the part of the studios.

In their heyday, though, the columnists existed on the highest plane of the publicity machine. Jimmy Fidler patterned himself after Walter Winchell—he had the same staccato *rat-tat-tat* verbal delivery and, like Winchell, was a presence on the radio, more so than any of the female columnists.

Fidler was so paranoid about his sources that if one of his informants called him, he identified himself by a code number rather than a name, just in case the line was tapped. Fidler was unusually frank, and would call out celebrities who he felt misbehaved. One day Errol Flynn decked him, which was a huge publicity boon, and Fidler went around town with a bodyguard for months afterward.

All these people had careers that lasted far longer than most stars. Hedda and Louella were still ruling the roost when I got into the movies after World War II, and they remained on the job until the 1960s.

Louella was a sweet, vague creature who lived for scoops and had only the dimmest idea of anything that went on outside of Hollywood. In April 1939, just after the Italians invaded Albania, and war was clearly looming on the horizon, she wrote, "The deadly dullness of the last week was lifted today when Darryl Zanuck admitted he had bought all rights to Maurice Maeterlinck's *The Blue Bird*."

The extent of my courting of Louella involved accompanying

That's me with Sophia Loren and Louella Parsons. On the far right is Clifton Webb.

her to the racetrack a few times. She had a special relationship with Fox because her husband "Docky" was the staff doctor at the studio.

There was nothing vague about Hedda Hopper, ever. She was a committed conservative who had forgone romantic entanglements after she divorced the stage star DeWolf Hopper in order to concentrate on raising her son, Bill, who would later play Paul Drake on the *Perry Mason* TV series. With Hedda as a mother, Bill's life could not have been easy, but in my opinion he turned out to be a very fine man.

Hedda's own acting career bottomed out in the 1930s, but in 1938 the *Los Angeles Times* tapped her to provide some competition for

Louella Parsons, who had been writing for the Hearst papers since
the silent days.

Hedda was a far more intimidating person than Louella, but it
was best not to mess with either of them. Both of them cultivated a
wide array of informants within the industry who, then as now,
tipped off the newspapers. If an actor sent flowers to an actress, the
florist could call Hedda or Louella and let her know that the parties
in question were having an affair, or were about to.

One of Hedda's great friends was Ida Koverman, who was Louis
B. Mayer's private secretary. It was Ida Koverman who brokered a
wide acceptance of Hedda among many of the stars and enabled
her to freshen her columns with up-to-date news and a more biting
attitude. Most of Hedda's best contacts were initially MGM stars
such as Jeanette MacDonald or Norma Shearer. Hedda started

A rare shot of the rival gossip columnists Hedda Hopper and Louella
Parsons, circa 1948.

attracting more attention, and consequently more papers, and she and Louella settled down to a feud that would continue for the next twenty-five years.

Very few people really liked either Hedda or Louella, but very few people could afford to make it obvious. Generally, the attitude the studios had toward them was public deference and nervous laughter behind their backs. Louella would come to the set to talk to you, but if Hedda wanted an interview, Mohammed had to go to the mountain. I went to her house several times over the years, usually lugging flowers and chocolates.

It was part of the game. You could get tired of it, but you couldn't show it. That's why they call it acting.

While it was primarily women who functioned as the pipeline to the public, the people who funneled the information to the pipeline— the heads of publicity at the studios—were all men: Howard Strickling at MGM and Harry Brand at Fox, among others. I knew Harry quite well, because I was signed to a contract at Fox in 1949.

Harry was born in 1896 in New York. When he was a child he broke his leg, but it was incorrectly set, leaving him with a slight limp for the rest of his life. Harry didn't come from the movie business, but from politics and journalism. He had worked with Howard Strickling at the *Los Angeles Express* and the *Los Angeles Tribune*, where they were both sportswriters. That trade will teach you the importance of winning and losing, and both Howard and Harry meant to be on the side of the winners. In fact, Harry always dressed more like a sportswriter than an executive in the movie industry— he wore a slouch hat.

After he left newspapers, Harry went to work for Warner Bros., then got hired by Joe Schenck at United Artists, where he even produced a couple of pictures. But Harry preferred publicity.

When Schenck joined forces with Darryl Zanuck to form 20th Century, which later merged with Fox, Harry became head of publicity there. By that time, he had been working with Joe Schenck for twelve years, and everybody in Hollywood knew and liked him.

Just about the same time as Schenck and Zanuck were joining forces, Harry joined forces with Sybil Morris, the daughter of a prominent Los Angeles family. Sybil and Harry were married in 1933. She was the right woman for him—idealistic, philanthropic, a doer. For a long time, Sybil's pet project was the Motion Picture Relief Fund, but years later she turned her interest toward rehabilitating female convicts. Sybil eventually raised more than eight million dollars for the Sybil Brand Institute for Women.

Because of Harry's background in journalism, he knew a lot of people who knew a lot of people—everyone from politicians and law enforcement officials (Harry's brother was a judge) to bartenders and racetrack touts. Sometimes Harry knew what was going on before the people who were involved did. Everybody liked him because he was genuinely likable; among his friends were both the ardent Democrat Harry Truman *and* the equally ardent Republican Richard Nixon (who loathed each other), not to mention a couple of governors and Supreme Court Chief Justice Earl Warren.

The influence of these publicity men eventually spread over the town. If journalism is all about figuring out who can give you the information you need for a story, the job of head of publicity at a movie studio is about figuring out how to keep the person who has the information from spilling it. Half the time, a press agent is really a suppress agent. In her memoirs Hedda Hopper wrote about how MGM spent nine thousand dollars keeping the reputation of one of its stars intact after he was caught propositioning an underage boy. Hopper didn't mention his name, but it was William

Haines. On those rare occasions when a star actually did make the papers for bad behavior—Robert Mitchum for smoking marijuana, Robert Walker or Frances Farmer for being drunk and disorderly—it was usually either a setup (Mitchum) or the studio washing its hands of a performer that was just too damn much trouble (Farmer).

Usually, though, every bar patronized by any actor knew that if an actor got drunk and disorderly, proper procedure involved calling the studio, not the cops. A publicist would show up quickly, some folding money would be exchanged, and the offender hustled away. If the star was actually taken in by the police, they in turn would call the studio and the star would be quietly taken home, with a corresponding standing order for a large batch of tickets for the next fund-raiser to the Police Athletic League. Charges were rarely brought.

The studios didn't believe they were exercising influence; they believed they were simply accepting favors from old friends. For a time Harry Brand even gave the dangerous gossip columnist Walter Winchell an office on the Fox lot, which made it unlikely that Winchell would write anything destructive about any of the stars.

Harry retired in 1962, in the middle of the *Cleopatra* debacle. The studio was pouring all its resources into the Rome location of the wildly overbudget epic, and the Fox publicity department was cut in half. (Not coincidentally, this was also the time when I made the decision to leave the studio, which focused on nothing but getting *Cleopatra* finished. Everything and everybody else had to fend for themselves, and I decided I could do better on my own, which indeed proved to be the case.)

Harry Brand died in 1989. He wanted no service, and requested that people who cared about him make a contribution to the Motion Picture and Television Country House and Hospital in

Press agent Harry Brand posing for a picture.

Woodland Hills. It was a typically generous gesture on the part of one of the genuinely good men of the movie industry, one who just happened to also know a great deal of the secret history of Hollywood.

As for Howard Strickling, he maintained his position with the people at MGM long after they, and he, had retired. It was Strickling who organized Spencer Tracy's funeral. Spence had left the studio a good dozen years before his death, and Howard was retired by then, but the family knew that only one man could organize the funeral in a way that Spence would have wanted. True to form, Howard kept the press away in a manner that didn't enrage them, and managed the entire day masterfully.

(That was typical of the people who had made up the MGM hierarchy: Kay Thompson, the vocal coach, was always on call to help out at MGM for years after she left the studio, and I believe Margaret Booth did a lot of "consulting" long after she was no longer the head of the MGM editorial department and had gone to work for Ray Stark.)

Another subculture that swarmed around the movie business consisted of press agents. One of the longest-serving, as well as one of the best, was Richard Gully. Richard was illegitimate, a cousin of Anthony Eden's, and extremely British. How he ended up in Hollywood I don't know, but Richard was involved in higher duties than just placing items in columns or keeping items out of them.

One of his gifts was introducing clients into Hollywood society. He worked for Jack Warner for a long time, and it was Richard who made a lady out of Ann Warner and a half-assed gentleman out of Jack. Richard knew everybody, and knew not only where all the bodies were buried, but what size shovels had been used. Yet he never said a word about any of it. My wife, Jill, adored him, as did most people who knew him.

These publicity men had to have their noses to the wind at all times; at the very least, they were street smart, and some of them were considerably more than that. Roughly speaking, their job could be divided into two parts: the nominal keeping of a star's name in front of the public, and crazed ballyhoo. The master of the latter was a man named Russell Birdwell, who masterminded David Selznick's search for Scarlett O'Hara, which made the entire nation even more conscious of *Gone with the Wind* than they would have ordinarily been.

Birdwell was a freelancer, and very expensive; he would charge a client as much as a hundred thousand dollars for a year of his services, plus overhead. He was brilliant but erratic. One day Carole Lombard heard a director complaining about the taxes he had to pay; she told him that, considering how much money she made, she felt that her tax bill was pretty reasonable. Birdwell promptly forwarded the remark to the IRS, which publicized it, and before you knew it Carole Lombard was being praised for her patriotism in being happy to pay her taxes.

It was Birdwell who devised the publicity campaign that promoted Jane Russell in *The Outlaw*, which centered almost completely on her chest, and who also handled the equally over-the-top campaign for John Wayne's *The Alamo*.

He likewise devised an innovative campaign for the Burt Lancaster film *Elmer Gantry*, having "Elmer Gantry was here" written all over sidewalks in Los Angeles and New York. The movie didn't have anything to do with sidewalks, or even with cities, but Birdwell inserted the movie's existence into the public's consciousness in a way that made him worth every penny he got.

In the early 1950s, when I became a star at Fox, the studio protected us very well. If a fan magazine was doing a feature, it was controlled by Fox. Back then, when Natalie and I went to our favorite restaurants, La Scala and Chasen's, there would often be guys standing outside asking if they could take a photograph. But it was all very well mannered, and we always let them shoot. It was nothing like it is now, with roving wolf packs of photographers and videographers trolling the streets of LA.

By the middle of the decade, though, the publicity business had begun to change. Before then, the studios wouldn't muscle Hedda or Louella, because they didn't have to; rather, they would finesse them. In return for keeping quiet about something the studio didn't want publicized, the columnists would be given a film for free for some charity show they were involved in. A couple of contractees would also be asked to attend and provide some star power. Between pleasing the studio and pleasing Hedda or Louella, it was a twofer.

Looking back, it was clearly a culture of back-scratching.

Hopper did have her pet hates, which she vented about often enough. She was particularly venomous about Charlie Chaplin's politics and bent for young girls, but Chaplin was an independent who prided himself on his independence, and didn't have the protection of a studio. If he had been under contract to a major studio, I can assure you Hopper would have criticized him in a more muted fashion.

But with the mid-1950s came the rise of magazines like *Confidential*, which the studios couldn't control. On top of that, the business was becoming decentralized, with the studios themselves now less important than the stars—a complete reversal of what Hollywood had been only twenty years before.

The rise of scandal sheets like *Confidential* meant that the studios had to learn to play defense. When *Confidential* was going to print a story about Rock Hudson's homosexuality, Rock's agent, Henry Willson, gave them Rory Calhoun instead—Calhoun had been busted for robbery as a juvenile—to protect Hudson, a far more important client. Most people thought that it had been Universal, the studio where both actors worked, who'd acted in this craven manner, but the culprit was even closer.

It was a simple calculation on Willson's part—10 percent of Rock's salary meant a lot more than 10 percent of Calhoun's.

Ultimately, it didn't make much difference. Willson, who was not only grossly unethical but unsavory as well, died broke. The relevant point here is that, twenty years earlier, or even ten, nobody would have dared print the truth about either actor.

While the monopoly that Jack Warner, Louis B. Mayer, and the rest of the founding moguls had enjoyed was disappearing, television was making serious inroads into movie attendance. This meant that fewer movies were being made, which in turn meant that the rosters of actors, writers, and directors under studio contracts were severely pared. More people began operating as freelancers, losing the protection of the studio as they did so. When both stars and studios lost control over publicity, they quickly discovered that power could disappear very quickly.

In the 1960s Kodak introduced the Instamatic, a light camera that fit in a pocket and used film cartridges that could be quickly switched, making picture taking easier than it had ever been before. I remember talking to Cary Grant once about the proliferation of new cameras, and he paused and said, "That's the end of celebrities."

He was speaking about a celebrity's loss of control of his or her own image. And he was right, although that loss involved a lot more than just the Instamatic.

The transition from an orderly process regarding publicity to the law of the jungle became obvious with Richard Burton, Elizabeth Taylor, and *Cleopatra*. I was in Rome when that film was being shot there, and that's all anybody talked about. Along the Via Veneto, the paparazzi *ignited*. And suddenly the paparazzi mattered more than they ever had, because for the first time there was real money at stake for the right picture of the illicit lovers together. That was the beginning.

Fifty years later, there are more stars than there used to be. Besides TV, there's cable, and then there are celebrities who don't do anything but be famous—the Kardashian sisters are the new Gabor sisters, but less amusing. There are also far more outlets for photographs of celebrities than there used to be, as the Internet has spawned countless gossip sites and blogs.

The shift in attitude is stunning. People used to be happy to see celebrities if they encountered them in public, and they were correspondingly pleasant. Going out to shop or get a meal was not a grueling run of the gauntlet. Very few photographers were allowed into the dining areas of restaurants or into hotels; unless a fan magazine set up a layout in advance at the Beverly Hills Hotel, you were in a zone of privacy.

Now photographers are looking for any opportunity to bust somebody, because that picture is worth so much. They're desperate to get shots of people drunk or angry, so they bait them, trying to provoke an incident. In so many ways it has become a culture of violation. It's true not just in show business, but in everything. If you're in politics, you're fair game as well.

A year or so ago Jodie Foster wrote an article whose central point was that, if she were a kid starting in the movie business today, she'd get out. According to her, it's just not worth it. I've begun to think that maybe she's right. If I were a young man today, I might just follow my father into business, and not the movie business.

I think that this adversarial relationship—the way that cameras shadow you every time you leave your house—is why a lot of celebrities have gotten out of Hollywood. George Clooney spends a great deal of his time in Italy; Brad Pitt and Angelina Jolie go to New Orleans or a château in France. There, the media are less viperous, and the celebrities have a greater ability to move around.

It's something I know all about. It's even worse when tragedy strikes.

Intellectually, I understand the perception that the rich and privileged are invincible. That's why some people need to believe, for example, that Marilyn Monroe was murdered by the Kennedys or Princess Diana was killed by the British royal family.

The documented facts—a long history of alcohol and narcotic abuse in the case of the former, a drunken chauffeur in the latter—seem insufficient. The randomness of life and death can be terrifying, so a certain kind of person seizes on minor discrepancies of memory or the garbled recollections of marginal personalities to cast doubt on a reality they don't want to acknowledge.

And you can never use facts or logic to argue somebody out of a position that fantasy got them into.

What's different is that our culture allows for these fantasies to be disseminated at will in real time. What's the line—"A lie can go halfway around the world before the truth puts its pants on"? Nowadays, a lie can go all the way around the world six times before you're even out of bed.

And the reality is that celebrities have to take it. Suing only gives the vipers the publicity they want and further incites the hungry hordes. As far as the celebrities are concerned, what starts out as suspicion can easily turn into hostility. In the twenty-first century, you are guilty until proven innocent, and for a lot of people you can never be proven innocent.

Let me illustrate: In May 1946, David Niven and his wife Primmie went to a party at Tyrone Power's house. Among the other guests were Rex Harrison, Lilli Palmer, Patricia Medina, and Richard Greene. After dinner they all took part in a hide-and-seek game called Sardines, which was played in the dark.

There was the sound of a door opening, and then a terrible, descending thud. Ty Power turned the lights on. Primmie Niven had mistaken the basement door for the bathroom door and taken a terrible fall down steps she hadn't realized were there. The fall was twenty feet, and she took it headfirst. She died two days later.

David and Primmie were a beloved part of Hollywood's English colony. The tragedy wasn't hushed up, but it didn't become common currency, either. David was devastated, but eventually remarried, a woman named Hjördis. The successes or failures of that marriage are irrelevant to the point I'm making, but let me say that I don't believe David was ever happy after that. He covered up his grief as gracefully as any man could have, but he was, deep down, broken-hearted.

Now, imagine that same accident happening in 2013. The gossip Web sites would go into overdrive. The tabloids would imply all manner of illicit goings-on at the party, and make inferences of an unhappy marriage leading to . . . *murder*—despite the fact that David was such a gentle soul that he would rescue bugs that had flown into his swimming pool.

But none of that would matter. The suspicions would be on page one, and the case being closed would be on page forty-eight—if it was printed at all. David and his sons would be hunted by video paparazzi every time they stepped out of their house. Proper grieving would be impossible. A terrible tragedy would be made even more traumatic. And it would never go away. Not really.

I shudder when I think about what David had to go through, but at least he had the small consolation of not having had his personal tragedy used for cheap media heroin.

From the time I was a young man about town and through my marriage to Natalie, I went to the store like a normal person. I mostly did my own shopping and bought my own groceries. I didn't think much about it at the time, but I think about it now, when I see videos of stores opening up after hours so an actress can buy some clothes. I don't remember any of the stars I knew having to do things like that back then.

Well, maybe one. When Natalie was seeing Elvis Presley, he would rent out an entire theater in Memphis to watch a movie. I always resisted affectations like that, because I wanted my kids to have as normal an environment as possible, and I think that kind of isolation can easily have very bad consequences.

I can honestly say that the only time going out in public became a problem was when we would take the kids to Disneyland. Then things could get pretty claustrophobic.

Today going to Disneyland would simply be impossible. Even going to the store like a normal person is something that's been taken away. Cameras and cell phones are ubiquitous.

Even when they're in New Orleans, Brad Pitt and Angelina Jolie have to bring security with them wherever they go. That strikes me as a very heavy price to pay for the benefits of celebrity. Among other things, you can no longer watch people, because they're all watching you. I think that can smother a young actor.

Of course, these days, that's the least of an actor's concerns.

Nightlife

The nightlife of Hollywood was slow to blossom for two reasons. First, the town was created as a haven for teetotalers. If that wasn't bad enough, along came Prohibition. It didn't stop movie people from drinking, but it did put a crimp in the ancillary businesses.

What happened in the early days of the movies was that nightclubs and bars simply opened outside the city limits of Hollywood in small towns like Vernon, Venice, or Culver City. Venice offered a place called the Three O'Clock Ballroom—named after closing time—that offered public dancing.

If you've ever seen Al Jolson's *The Jazz Singer*, you might remember that the first musical number in the film takes place at a dive called Coffee Dan's. This was a huge in-joke, because there actually was a Coffee Dan's in downtown Los Angeles. It was in an alley on Hill, between Seventh and Eighth, and you entered the place by sliding down a chute into the subterranean recesses of a place that was designed to look like a Paris boîte, complete with Apache dancers. There was jazz, and I can't imagine there wasn't booze, too.

A lot of these places were run by a man named Baron Long—a great name for a bootlegger—who was the same man who'd dreamed up Agua Caliente. Long was originally a boxing promoter who put on matches in Vernon, which also had a bar owned by a promoter, Jack Doyle. It wasn't long before Vernon became the go-to place for people in the movie colony who wanted to eat, drink, and make merry—or Mary.

The legend goes that Southern California first heard jazz at the Vernon Country Club, where Paul Whiteman played the violin. "Vernon Country Club" sounds lofty, but it was nothing but a glorified roadhouse situated among beet fields.

From the alcohol intake around Hollywood, you never would have known it was Prohibition during those years. In downtown Los Angeles there were a couple of fashionable places serving what I was told was excellent-quality bootleg alcohol. Among them were Al Levy's Café and Mike Lyman's Sunset Inn, the latter of which was near the ocean in Pacific Palisades, right around the corner from where I lived for twenty-five years.

There were about twenty speakeasies within the bounds of Hollywood proper in the twenties, which doesn't even take into account the independent operators who ran around the studios procuring a bottle or two for certain actors, writers, and directors. Louis B. Mayer's favorite bootlegger was Frankie Orsatti, who was the brother of the baseball player Ernie Orsatti. Frank became a major agent around town long after his bootlegging days were over. (The movie industry was a blue-collar trade for several generations, and I leave it up to you to decide who made better movies—the tough guys who talked out of the side of their mouths, or the college boys.)

I heard tell of a Frenchman named Maurice who was a caterer by profession but who offered a lot more than pigs in a blanket. Along Hollywood Boulevard were two bookstores catty-corner across from each other: Stanley Rose and Larry Edmunds. The writers patronized them en masse, so Rose and Edmunds kept them supplied with booze. (Larry Edmunds's shop is still there, a block or so away from where it used to be, the last bookstore of what used to be a thriving ten or so around Hollywood Boulevard. But don't get your hopes up—all they sell now is books and movie stills.) The major bootlegger of this period is said to have been one Tony Cornero, who could supply gin, bourbon, and grappa. For scotch and rum, the pickings were slimmer, because they're harder to make.

Baron Long also owned the Sunset Inn, which was just below the bluffs of Santa Monica and was hugely popular for its dancing contests. Abe Lyman played there; Harold Lloyd and Bebe Daniels, his costar and girlfriend, were always winning the dancing trophies.

Baron Long also introduced what would become a primary building block of Hollywood restaurants: art direction. He built the Ship Café in Venice, a floating Spanish galleon that also served as a hotel. The waiters were outfitted as sixteenth-century naval officers. If you could afford a drink, they'd pour you one, Prohibition be damned.

The Ship Café underwent several name and management changes over the years, but it hung on until shortly after World War II. By that time Prohibition was long gone, and the novelty restaurants had shifted much closer to Hollywood.

However much Hollywood had to offer in terms of entertainment, it had only a handful of really good restaurants. With few exceptions Los Angeles didn't become a great restaurant town until after World War II. A great restaurant, which is to say a restaurant where the experience is equal to the food, is a lot like theater: you have to establish a mood, and you hope to attract some players who will set off the experience with a certain dramatic power.

When Hollywood was being settled, the people who were living in the Spanish Revival houses generally kept to simple fare when dining out. Charlie Chaplin and Douglas Fairbanks favored Musso & Frank on Hollywood Boulevard, which was founded in 1919. By the 1930s Musso's had become the unofficial headquarters for the writers in town, and you'd find William Faulkner, F. Scott Fitzgerald, and Nathanael West there when they were in town trying to make some money so they could afford to write their novels. Amazingly, it is still in business, a block or two from its original site, but with much the same menu that it had ninety years ago—steak and fish, superbly prepared.

Chaplin financed a restaurant on Hollywood Boulevard a block or two from Musso's called Henry's, where he was a regular customer. It was run by Henry Bergman, a bald, round member of the Chaplin stock company who served as a sort of court jester for the comedian. Henry's was long gone by the time I got into the business—for that matter, so was Henry Bergman, who had died a few years earlier—but a surviving copy of its menu shows that Chaplin's culinary taste was basic. That wasn't unusual—even a place as well known as the Brown Derby could be classified as home style, specializing in comfort foods like meat loaf and corned beef hash.

Another interesting restaurant—a minor legend, in fact—was Victor Hugo, which was originally on Hill Street downtown but later moved to Beverly Drive in Beverly Hills. Victor Hugo was an all-you-can-eat place and, like all such establishments, was heavy on carbohydrates. For a dollar fifty your lunch consisted of a selection drawn from enchiladas, goulash, spaghetti, glazed tongue, salads, rolls, eggs, chicken à la king, or ravioli. Dessert consisted of French pastries and strawberry cakes. Dinner would run as much as five dollars—a lot of money for a meal in those days, and enough to keep the tourists out.

In 1937 Lucius Beebe, who wrote sniffy stories for the slick magazines, published a piece for *Scribner's Magazine* in which he described the restaurant manners of Hollywood folk as appalling. He took particular exception to the habit of placing telephones at the tables, which was the height of chic for about twenty years. He found it ostentatious, which it was. On the other hand, decisions regarding the expenditure of millions of dollars couldn't always wait. These days, kids think nothing of answering their cell phones at dinner to talk about nothing at all.

And that will be one of the few you-kids-get-off-my-lawn remarks that I will make in this book.

Another thing Beebe objected to was serving each member of a party individually, for the convenience of late arrivals. Serving a late arrival his appetizer while another member of the party might already be working on his entrée seems to me a commonsense arrangement for a working town where very few people punched a nine-to-five clock.

But Beebe was right about one thing: service was predicated on your social standing. The more important you were, or the better friend you were of the proprietor, the better your table and the more attentive the service. Although I suspect that that was also a way to keep tourists out.

Most of the restaurants of that era were centered on Hollywood Boulevard, because that's where most of the studios were. Famous Players–Lasky, soon to change its name to Paramount, was on Vine Street; Warner Bros. was down on Sunset. Of the large studios, only Goldwyn was an outlier, far away in Culver City.

But there was more to the Hollywood dining experience than

the meal itself; part of it was simply being seen, and usually on the studio's dime. Most of the Hollywood restaurants allowed a handful of photographers to snap shots of the elite dining. It was good for the restaurant and it was thought to be good for the stars, although having flashbulbs pop in your face when you'd really rather be eating was the sort of minor irritant that was part of the job.

One of the forgotten names of Old Hollywood is Eddie Brandstatter, who ran several nightclubs around town. In 1922 he opened the Café Montmartre on Hollywood Boulevard. The Montmartre was on the second floor of a building down the street from Musso & Frank and held 350 patrons in a luxurious environment that was unusual for that period. Brandstatter had outfitted it with chandeliers from Czechoslovakia, Belgian carpets, and what was advertised as 2,400 pounds of sterling silver.

During the silent days, it was the place to go; Gloria Swanson, Rudolph Valentino, John Barrymore, and Marion Davies all ate there regularly. When luminaries such as Winston Churchill and Prince George of England came to Hollywood, they were taken to the Montmartre as a matter of course.

It was at the Montmartre where the practice of people hovering outside the front door for autographs first became popular—a practice that still goes on today at popular nightspots around town. The Montmartre closed in 1929, reopened, then closed again. Those years in the 1920s were its height.

Eddie Brandstatter moved on and opened several new places, one right next door to the Montmartre. This was the Embassy Club, which opened in 1930 and was a private establishment limited to three hundred members who were meant to be, and apparently were, the crème de la crème of Hollywood society.

The Embassy's board of directors included Marion Davies,

Norma Talmadge, Constance Talmadge, John Gilbert, King Vidor, and Sid Grauman. A blend of Byzantine and Spanish styles, the club was designed by Carl Jules Weyl, who became an art director at Warner Bros. The main feature was a glass-enclosed rooftop lounge that offered a great view of the Hollywood Hills.

The only problem was that the Embassy Club was *so* exclusive that it couldn't make any money and went bankrupt. A few years later Brandstatter opened another club, this time on Hollywood right near Vine. It was called Sardi's, not to be confused with the famous theatrical Sardi's in New York.

The Hollywood Sardi's was designed by Rudolph Schindler in a stylish Moderne. Schindler first came to Los Angeles to supervise the construction of the Hollyhock House for Frank Lloyd Wright. After that commission was completed, he stayed and became a leading architectural modernist, probably most famous for his own house on Kings Road.

As at the Montmartre, dinner was served at Sardi's, but the emphasis was on lunch—noiseless wagons full of hors d'oeuvres were pushed around the tables, the way dim sum is today.

For a time restaurants in Hollywood had a way of looking like movie sets, in the spirit of Baron Long's Ship Café. The Brown Derby was shaped like a huge hat. Its cofounder Wilson Mizner was a wit and occasional screenwriter. His brother, Addison, was the architect who brought the Mediterranean Revival style, so popular in Southern California, to the East Coast, specifically Florida. Both of the Mizner brothers were rogues, and supposedly Addison had to get out of Florida after being implicated in a land swindle. It was only a short hop from there to writing scripts in Hollywood.

The story goes that one night at the Ambassador Hotel, Herbert Somborn, who had just divorced Gloria Swanson and was flush with alimony, was sitting with Mizner and Sid Grauman. Mizner casually observed that the area was not exactly filled to the brim with fine eating establishments, and ventured that if someone actually managed to provide good food, "people would probably come to eat it out of a hat." Another version says that Mizner modeled the place after the headgear worn by the two men he most admired: Bat Masterson and Alfred E. Smith.

Maybe.

What everybody does agree on was Jack Warner's accurate assessment of the problem: there was no "really first-class restaurant where actors of lofty eminence could dine in relative privacy."

Actually, Jack Warner didn't talk like that—he never used a phrase like "lofty eminence" in his life. Jack Warner's press agents talked like that. Whoever said it, the opinion behind the sentence was true.

The land for the Derby came from Somborn, who had invested some of his Swanson settlement on property across from the Ambassador Hotel. Wilson Mizner supplied the decorating, while the atmosphere, and the money, I believe, came from Jack Warner.

The original Brown Derby, at 3427 Wilshire Boulevard, was a hit from the day it opened in 1926—partly because the food was good, and partly because it stayed open till four a.m. Drunks, insomniacs, and night owls could always find somebody to talk to there, even if it was only a bartender. Somborn had an eye for the ladies and made sure to hire very attractive waitresses—I was told that some of the girls who waited tables early on came from the Ziegfeld Follies.

The Derby held only a hundred people and wasn't really much to look at. Booths ran along the walls, and above each one hung a light fixture in the shape of a brown derby.

The exterior facade of the Brown Derby on Wilshire.

Wilson Mizner hung out in Booth 50 for the next seven years, until his death. He became legendary for insulting the people who hired him. "You were sixty years old before you knew what a bathtub was," was one bomb he dropped on a producer. Once, when Douglas Fairbanks complained that his table was tilted, Mizner retorted, "How can you expect anything in Hollywood to be on the level?"

The regulars at Mizner's booth included Darryl Zanuck, W. C. Fields, John Barrymore, Anita Loos, and a phalanx of lesser screenwriters. Mizner thought anybody who hired him had to be a sucker, and the fact that they kept hiring him only proved it.

The Derby became such a touchstone for the town's fashionable that Darryl Zanuck once said, "If you make a bad picture it's very doubtful that you'll get a good table at the Brown Derby." But everybody makes a bad picture now and then, and in any case the

Photofest

The famous booths at the Brown Derby.

front booth at the Hollywood Derby was always reserved for studio heads: Harry Cohn, Jack or Harry Warner, and, yes, Zanuck.

On Valentine's Day in 1929, the restaurant added a second location, on Vine Street, which became even more popular because it was close to Columbia and Paramount. The Vine Street Derby sat two hundred, and its waitstaff was all male, in pressed uniforms. The booths had low backs, so everybody could see everybody else, which made working the room easier.

For years the Vine Street Derby was open twenty-four hours a day, seven days a week, and the elite customers—William Powell, Joan Crawford, Kate Hepburn—sat in booths on the north side of the building, underneath caricatures of them that were originally done by an artist named Eddie Vitch. That delightful custom began in 1933, when Vitch stopped in and offered to draw caricatures in exchange for food. The manager pointed to a couple of celebrities that happened to be dining, and Vitch quickly captured their essence in a few broad strokes.

After Vitch returned to Europe, the job of drawing the caricatures was taken over by a man known only as Zel. Supposedly, nobody knew his full name. Zel would complete his drawing, the subject would autograph it, and it would be hung on the wall. The caricatures became a barometer of status. Agents would try to have their clients' pictures hung next to legends like Gable and Cooper; occasionally the drawings had to be rearranged because marriages broke up.

The value of those pieces would be staggering today.

I'd say the restaurant got the best of that particular exchange.

The Derby eventually became a central part of Hollywood life. Wallace Beery ate there all the time, usually ordering the corned beef hash, with sponge cake drenched in ketchup (!) for dessert. Joe E. Brown liked the hash, too. Tom Mix always ordered the bouillabaisse.

The Vine Street Derby was also designed by Carl Weyl, who went on to be a success in the movies, too, winning Oscars for art directing *The Adventures of Robin Hood* and *Casablanca*. In fact, in the latter Weyl gave Bogart an office above Rick's Café that looked a lot like Bob Cobb's office in the Brown Derby.

Bob Cobb was a presence at the restaurant for what seemed like forever, from the late 1920s to his death in 1970. Cobb was a Montana man who wore cowboy boots when he was in the mood, but the rest of the time was impeccably outfitted. (Bob never lost his affinity for cowboys; one of his closest friends was Tom Mix, and Bob always said that he was the last person to hear from Mix before his fatal car accident in 1940. "Coming home," cabled Mix. "Meet you at the Derby.")

That said, informality extended only so far with Bob. Although the Derby was basically a steakhouse, proprieties were observed—not only were the waiters well turned out, but the patrons wore ties. (There were exceptions; I've seen a photo of Charlie Chaplin eating at the Derby without a tie, but then he was Charlie Chaplin. I never saw anybody without a tie in the restaurant itself, at least not while Bob was alive.)

In the beginning Bob was just the manager, but when Somborn died in 1934, just a few months after Wilson Mizner passed away, Bob took over the operation and made it an even greater success. He spent his life at the Derby, and he welcomed people of a similar commitment. The maître d' was Bill Chilias, who reigned at the Hollywood Derby from 1929 to 1955, and a jack of all trades was Benny Massi, who was there on opening day and stayed for the next forty-six years.

A maître d' at a major Hollywood restaurant has to have the diplomatic skills of a secretary of state; Bill always made sure that everybody had reservations, and he also made sure that the best booths were held for the best customers. Being a maître d' at a major Hollywood restaurant is also a lucrative business; Bill would make thousands of dollars in tips at Christmastime alone.

In the beginning the Derby served food that could have come out of a lunch wagon: hot dogs, grilled cheese sandwiches, hamburgers, chili. When Bob Cobb took it over, it got better fast, although its menu was never elaborate. The beef came from the East, the lobsters from Maine, the bacon from Canada; the cream in the coffee was heavy, and the Catalina sand dabs you ate at night had usually been harvested that morning. The prices were not cheap for the period, but there were lots of places that were much more expensive. The Derby charged thirty cents for an average cocktail, and a house specialty, such as the Bamboo, would run forty cents.

But Bob's greatest invention went far beyond the confines of the Brown Derby. The Cobb salad came about because Bob was hungry, but not for any of the overly familiar—to him, anyway—items on the menu.

Late one night, he threw together a chopped salad of chicken and a variety of other leftover ingredients. Some friends dropped in as Bob was eating and asked what the delicious-looking dish was. They tried it, they liked it . . . and millions of others have tried and liked the Cobb salad since. Yet I've tasted versions that would have greatly surprised Bob, who placed the emphasis on avocados, Roquefort cheese, and his own homemade French dressing.

During the Depression, Bob had to be economical; he even figured out a use for his day-old bread, by devising pumpernickel cheese toast. Bob made his own delicious coleslaw, which was served inside the sandwiches, not on the side. Also excellent was his homemade Thousand Island dressing, which had a kick to it—Bob mixed in chili sauce and bell peppers, as well as capers.

Besides his restaurants, Bob loved baseball. In 1938, when a Triple-A franchise in the Pacific Coast League became available, Bob invested in what would become the Hollywood Stars, who were popular for years; he was joined in the venture by Bing Crosby, Cecil B. DeMille, Walt Disney, Gary Cooper, George Burns, Robert Taylor, and Barbara Stanwyck. Years later, Bob helped bring the Dodgers to Los Angeles. Sorry, Brooklyn.

The huge success of the first two Derbies spawned two more: one that opened in 1931 in Beverly Hills on the corner of Wilshire and Rodeo, and another that opened in 1941 in Los Feliz.

The latter had a large carhop area that enabled people to dine in their autos.

Bob was now a restaurant mogul, and he enjoyed it to the hilt. He took especially good care of George Raft, who was there all the time, especially after his career cratered in the 1950s and he got into terrible tax trouble. George was on his ass, but Bob always reserved a booth with a phone for him, so George could have his meals while waiting for nonexistent job offers.

One day at the Brown Derby George told me he was working on a memoir. I told him that I had his title, and that he didn't have to give me anything for it. "Call it 'Heads or Tails,'" I said, referring to the great coin flipping bit he had done in *Scarface*, which started his career. George nodded and thanked me. When the book came out, it was called *The George Raft Story*. I still think my title was better.

The wives of the restaurateurs were often on hand in all the prime Hollywood eateries, because a restaurant takes more than one person to run it. Most of the wives were primary contributors to their respective husbands' successes, and thus it became their success as well. Bob Cobb's wife Sally was a very pleasant woman. Besides the Brown Derby empire, she helped Bob run the glass-bottom boat concession around Catalina for years.

Bob became something of a showman, as a restaurateur has to be. He had an ice sculpture created daily for the Vine Street Derby, for instance; on Fridays, it would be of two boxers. On those Fridays that branch of the restaurant would be packed for early dinner. Friday night was boxing night, and the Vine Street Derby was just a short walk from the Hollywood Legion Stadium, where the fights were held.

Among the regular attendees of those Friday night matches

were the Irish mafia: Pat O'Brien, Jimmy Cagney, Spencer Tracy, Frank McHugh, and Ralph Bellamy. Mae West was also a great fan of boxing—or, more likely, of boxers. If you wanted to eat at the Brown Derby on Vine, you were sure to get a table anytime after seven forty-five on Friday night, because the place would clear out as if someone had sounded a fire alarm.

After the fights were over, the place rapidly filled up again. It was like the tide going out, then coming back in.

People talk about careers being started at Schwab's Pharmacy, but a lot of careers began at the Brown Derby as well. George Raft, for instance, was spotted there in 1930 by Rowland Brown, a director at Fox. Brown told Raft to come over to the studio for a test, and he nabbed the part of Spencer Tracy's bodyguard in a movie called *Quick Millions*, which, in turn, led to his being cast in *Scarface*.

I was told that Clark Gable proposed to Carole Lombard at the Derby, and I'd like to think it's true. Certainly, my own connection with the Brown Derby was momentous. Right before Natalie Wood and I were married on December 28, 1957, we had dinner there, then took off for Scottsdale, where we had our ceremony performed so as to get away from our studios' attempts at stage managing. There's even a picture of us there that was taken very close to that night. I'm on the phone (sorry!), sitting under artwork of Joan Crawford and Olivia de Havilland. Natalie is looking at me like a woman in love, which, God knows, we were.

Hollywood in the 1970s was no place for class, and so the Vine Street Derby fell on hard times. It managed to continue operating until 1985, when it closed for reconstruction because of earthquake damage. A few years later it finally closed for good, and was demolished in 1994. Today, there's a splendid reconstruction of the original Brown Derby at Disney World in Florida, complete with reproductions of the original sketches by Vitch.

Somehow, I think Bob and Sally Cobb would be pleased.

The main growth area for the second generation of Hollywood restaurants was Sunset Boulevard. Supposedly the first nightclub on what became the Strip was a place called Maxine's, at 9103 Sunset, right around the corner from an avocado orchard. (In the '20s, the far end of Sunset Boulevard was a poinsettia field.)

In the early 1930s a place called La Boheme opened. It looked vaguely French, like a large roadside inn. The food was supposedly good, but it was largely a gambling establishment. In 1934 La Boheme became the Trocadero—one of the landmarks of Hollywood nightlife.

The Trocadero was the brainchild of Billy Wilkerson, the founder and publisher of the *Hollywood Reporter* and one of the town's great rogues. Billy had founded the *Hollywood Reporter* in 1930, and quickly became one of Hollywood's most outspoken figures. Whether scolding or boosting, he was always vehement. He blackmailed studios into supporting the paper with ads. If they didn't advertise in the proportions he considered proper, he simply blackballed them from coverage, from press releases to film reviews.

The studios didn't take this lying down, and would fight back by interfering with the distribution of the paper. There were several times when Billy was on the verge of going under, but he was always rescued by a timely loan from one of his friends, like Joe Schenck or Howard Hughes.

Billy sensed that the Sunset Strip was something special. Its beauty was that it was an unincorporated zone, a no-man's-land. It

Portrait of Billy Wilkerson.

didn't belong to either Hollywood or Beverly Hills, but was perfectly situated in between. In practice, this meant that it was more or less wide open for booze during Prohibition and gambling at any time. It was Billy Wilkerson who made the area between Crescent Heights Boulevard and Doheny Drive the swankiest place on the Strip.

After Prohibition was repealed, Billy kicked into high gear. He began importing wines and liquor and needed a place for storage. That was when he came across the building on the Strip that had once been La Bohème. He bought it mainly because it had a large cellar, then decided to convert the upstairs into a nightclub. That abandoned place ultimately became the Trocadero.

Billy didn't have a lot of money, but he did have an endless supply of hustle, so he convinced Harold Grieve, the husband of silent screen star Jetta Goudal and a good designer, to decorate the place in return for deferred payments. Grieve went along with it.

But Billy was still running short, and just before the Trocadero's opening, he saw Myron Selznick driving by and invited him in. He asked Selznick why he had never thrown a party.

Before they were through talking, Selznick agreed to have the opening night party at the Trocadero, which tided Wilkerson over until the money came rolling in afterward. (There was a persistent rumor that what Selznick got in return for his largesse was persistently kind treatment in the pages of the *Hollywood Reporter* for all of his clients. I wasn't there, but it sounds like a fair exchange, Hollywood-style.)

The Trocadero was familiarly known as The Troc. It was a low, colonial-style building that had a long striped canopy. It was more of a social place, a place to meet and greet, than a genuinely good restaurant. The Troc had a maître d' named Jean, who was a wizard of protocol, always juggling tables and booths so that nobody's feelings were hurt.

That same year, a far less imposing but ultimately more long-lasting institution opened on La Brea: the Farmers Market. At the time, it was just an empty lot owned by an oil company that began attracting tailgaters who sold produce out of the back of their trucks. But it grew until it became one of the most delightful places in town—you can still get a great breakfast there.

My second wife Marion's mother was one of the three original waitresses at Dupar's at the Farmers Market, and she overheard lots of juicy Hollywood gossip while waiting tables. In the early days of Dupar's, she won a raffle and had her choice of first prizes: a lot far out on Ventura Boulevard or a turkey. Since Ventura Boulevard was little more than a goat path at the time, she chose the turkey, and nobody questioned her decision. A true story, one she never tired of telling.

Years later Marion was in a scene with me in *Halls of*

Montezuma, the first movie in which I got billing. More than ten years after that, Marion and I were married. It's amazing how often life closes into a circle.

World War II changed Hollywood, and for those four years there was a perceptible sense of economic expansion in the air. Hollywood itself was at full employment, as were the aircraft and shipping industries that were both based on the West Coast.

After Pearl Harbor more than a thousand actors, technicians, directors, and writers beat a path to the enlistment offices to sign up, including some of the biggest stars in the business: Clark Gable, James Stewart, Robert Taylor, Tyrone Power. So did some of the men who ran the studios—Darryl Zanuck went off to war, and William Goetz took over Fox for the duration.

Patriotism exploded. The Hollywood Canteen opened up at 1451 Cahuenga, just south of Sunset. The Canteen was spearheaded by Bette Davis and John Garfield, and funded by money from Ciro's and Harry Cohn. The property had originally been the site of a joint called the Barn, and all of the Hollywood unions donated material and workers to convert the place. The stars did their part, too—Cary Grant bought a piano, Jack Warner donated linoleum. By the time the Canteen opened in October 1942, it was a very comfortable nightclub with a western theme.

The Canteen opened at six p.m. and closed at midnight. If you were in the service and on leave in California, the Canteen would be your first stop. Soldiers were admitted free of charge, and I remember seeing throngs of them waiting outside by five p.m. Close to twelve hundred men would crowd into the place. John Ford's wife ran the kitchen. Male stars bused tables, and female stars danced with the soldiers. The music was provided by a rotation of name bands that donated their time. When the band wasn't

Ginny Simms entertaining the troops at the Hollywood Canteen.

playing, comedians and dancers would get up onstage and do their thing.

The Canteen was an experiment in community mobilization and it was a complete success. It lasted until the end of the war, and I like what it says about the best instincts of people in show business. Some stars showed up only for photo ops, but there were many who took their duties seriously. Marlene Dietrich was there a lot, as was Frances Langford.

The first March of Dimes fund-raising event during World War II massed at Hollywood and Vine, and the turnout was so huge it stopped traffic. The Red Car that ran down the middle of Hollywood Boulevard couldn't move. I know—I was stuck there for more than an hour.

Red Skelton mugs it up while Spencer Tracy carves a Thanksgiving turkey for the soldiers at the Hollywood Canteen.

In other areas patriotism stopped at the studio door. The war years meant many sacrifices for the rest of the country, but they were comfortable for Hollywood. Although "rationing" became one of the keywords of the war, when it came to the stars and the people who presented them, those restrictions didn't apply. Within the studios you could get nylons, gas, filet mignons, and other goods that the rest of America could only dream about.

Movie attendance during this era exploded, reaching as high as 90 million people a week—this in a country whose total population was about 135 million. Everyone was going to the movies.

After the war, the Hollywood social scene slowly began to change, although many nightclubs remained on and around the Sunset Strip. Ciro's, Billy Wilkerson's other great success, was still

Bette Davis serving cigarettes to the boys.

a place to go in the 1950s. It opened at 8433 Sunset, the heart of the Strip, at the end of January 1940 and immediately became a magnet for stars and heavyweights in the industry. As always, Wilkerson gave his nightclub a luxurious setting befitting a Hollywood movie. The walls were draped in ribbed silk dyed a pale green, and the ceiling was painted the muted red of an American Beauty rose. There were sofas along the walls, with silk coverings dyed to match the ceiling. The lighting fixtures were custom made in the shape of bronze columns and urns.

Ciro's was less of a spectacular dining experience than it was a place to be seen, and it remained that way for the duration of its existence. Billy Wilkerson wasn't there very long; he had a low threshold of boredom and bailed out after a couple of years, but

Abbe Lane outside of Ciro's nightclub.

Ciro's lived on. It was at Ciro's that I saw Kay Thompson and the Williams Brothers—the best nightclub act I have ever seen in my life. Andy Williams was more than good by himself, but with his brothers, Dick, Bob, and Don, he was great. I miss Andy—he was a good friend.

In that era most nightclub acts were basically static; the performer stood at the microphone or sat at the piano, and that was that. But Kay and the Williams Brothers were in constant motion, which was made possible by a series of overhead microphones. Their chemistry was palpable, and the act was precisely staged and choreographed by Robert Alton, who had worked with Thompson at MGM.

Then there was the Mocambo, which was a few doors down from

the Trocadero on the Sunset Strip. The Trocadero had a great view of the low-lying area south of the Strip, but the Mocambo, which opened at 8588 Sunset on January 3, 1941, had that and a little bit extra besides. Its décor was commonly described as a cross between a somewhat decadent Imperial Rome, Salvador Dalí, and a birdcage.

The color scheme was soft blue, terra-cotta, and silver, and along the walls were paintings by Jane Berlandina, as well as huge tin flowers. The columns were a flaming red—that sounds like Dalí—covered with paintings of harlequins. As for the birdcage, that referred to a long glass aviary that was alive with dozens of brilliantly colored parrots and macaws. To my knowledge, it was the only public aviary in Los Angeles, and it attracted a lot of attention, although initially local animal lovers petitioned to have the birds

The swanky Mocambo nightclub on the Sunset Strip in June 1951. The table in the center hosts a dinner party thrown by gossip columnist Louella Parsons.

A pretty girl excited for a fun night at the Mocambo.

protected from all the nightclub noise. Charlie Morrison, one of the owners, agreed to install thick curtains around the aviary during the day so the birds could get some rest. The Mocambo, along with Ciro's, was one of the premier nightspots for twenty years—a very long run in a transient business.

In all the first-class Sunset Boulevard nightclubs, jackets and ties were required for the men, and slacks weren't allowed for women. Likewise, unescorted men and women were discouraged, probably to minimize the presence of hustlers. Which is not to say that nothing untoward went on. A lot of women would arrive with a bevy of male escorts, and often one man would enter with several women. They would then split up, and it was every man and woman for him- or herself.

The Mocambo had a bandleader named Emil, who would

always strike up "That Old Black Magic" whenever Bogart and Bacall walked in. Interestingly these clubs were integrated long before the rest of America, at least as far as the entertainment went. Hazel Scott played the Mocambo for years, as did the Nat King Cole Trio.

The heyday of the Trocadero—at 8610 Sunset or, as Billy Wilkerson's ads had it, "Boulevard de Sunset"—was in the thirties and forties. When I started going there in the 1950s, it was still a special place, as were all of the fabled clubs on that part of the strip.

Certainly, it was full of special people. Everybody went to the Troc, from moguls like Sam Goldwyn and his wife, to the invariably unattached Joe Schenck, to directors like William Wellman and stars like Bing Crosby and William Powell. Marlene Dietrich was a regular, as was Louis B. Mayer, who liked to go dancing there in the interim between divorcing his first wife—a pleasant, slightly dull woman he had married in Boston decades before—and marrying his second—the glamorous widow of a William Morris agent.

The Troc was one of the few clubs where Fred Astaire would be seen. Fred didn't go out much, because his wife Phyllis was shy and didn't like what Satchel Paige referred to as "the social ramble." Since Fred adored Phyllis, he was perfectly happy to stay close to home. Avoiding nightclubs was also a good way of avoiding the women who would beg Fred to dance with them. Just as mail carriers aren't enthusiastic about taking walks on their days off, Fred didn't particularly care for social dancing.

The Trocadero certainly didn't look like much from the outside, but Harold Grieve successfully converted the interior into a stylish French café, and in keeping with the décor, the menu was French as well.

The walls were painted cream, and there was a touch of gold in the molding and the striped silk chairs. Many people in the

A rare shot of Mr. and Mrs. Astaire, photographed along with Robert Montgomery, during an evening meal at the Trocadero.

industry believed that the Troc kicked off Hollywood's great period of off-screen glamour.

I remember that one of the highlights of the place was a wall-size mural of Paris as glimpsed from the Sacré-Coeur. In front of the mural there was a real railing on which rested a pot of fresh flowers. The illusion, especially in dim light, was quite lovely.

The Trocadero was expensive—drinks began at sixty cents and went all the way up to a dollar fifty for something called the French 75 (which sounds like a condom). The house special was the Trocadero Cooler, which cost seventy-five cents. (For context, two filet mignons at the Cocoanut Grove would set you back $14.50 in 1937 dollars, or not much less than the average weekly paycheck.)

Billy Wilkerson had a showman's knack for innovation. Sundays were traditionally a dead night in the nightclub business in

Hollywood, because people had to be at work early on Monday morning. So Billy started what amounted to an open-mike night, where young talent could perform. The result was that Sunday night at the Troc ultimately became nearly as popular as Saturday, as movers and shakers began to feel obliged to attend, lest some other studio sign a brilliant young comic or dancer.

The Trocadero was enormously influential, and other clubs tried to get in on its success by opening on or around Sunset Boulevard. At the height of the Sunset Strip—just before, during, and after World War II—Mocambo, the Trocadero, La Rue, and the Crillon were all within a few blocks of one another; if you went to one, chances are you'd go to a couple of others for a drink or a nightcap.

Although they presented some of the same acts, these clubs were not really analogous to the nightclub culture of New York City. They had a different clientele, and I found them more personalized than the clubs of New York. Mainly, they seemed less formal. On the Strip you could just drop in after dinner to catch a wonderful act; most of the places had a cover charge, but it was often waived for celebrities.

There were, of course, clubs that offered more than a meal and conventional entertainment. On Harold Way was a place called Club Mont-Aire, which offered pleasures of the fleshly variety. Several doors away from the Mont-Aire was a house run by one of Hollywood's legendary madams, a lady—I have been assured by several of her loyal customers that she was, in fact, a lady—named Brenda Allen, whose outfit was finally closed down by the vice squad in 1948.

Radio had become increasingly important to the local economy in the early 1930s, and both NBC and CBS built large radio studios within a few hundred yards of each other. NBC was at the intersection of Sunset and Vine, and CBS was on Sunset east of Vine.

The hundreds of people who worked for the two companies meant that there was a surge of restaurants around the area. The Brown Derby was already there, but it wasn't long before it was joined by Sardi's, the Coco Tree Café, Mike Lyman's, La Conga, and a couple of fast-food drive-ins.

Of all the restaurants that opened around World War II, I remember Romanoff's most fondly. It was run, of course, by the man who called himself Prince Michael Romanoff. Everybody knew that he wasn't really "a cousin of the late Czar," as he liked to proclaim (though not too insistently), but nobody seemed too sure about who he really was. Apparently Mike Romanoff was actually Harry Gerguson, the son of a Cincinnati tailor, although the mystery of his origins persists to this day. In any other town but Hollywood, that sort of impersonation would be considered reprehensible, if not actionable, but in Hollywood it's called . . . *acting*.

Mike was such a charismatic man! The story went that he enlisted Harry Crocker, a very well-connected friend of Charlie Chaplin's and a columnist for the Hearst papers, to finagle seventy-five hundred dollars each from a bunch of movie people as seed money for a restaurant. Among the investors were Robert Benchley, Cary Grant, Darryl Zanuck, and John Hay Whitney, the latter of whom had also bankrolled Selznick International. Supposedly, Jack Warner also put up some money, and Jack and Darryl were not exactly bosom buddies.

By the time I met Mike in the late 1940s, he was a prince of the realm—impeccably trimmed mustache, with spats and a cane. He

Bettmann/CORBIS

Mike Romanoff in front of his eponymous restaurant.

lived in hotels, he borrowed money from everybody, usually paid it back, and was incredibly charming. Despite his name, he didn't attempt a fake Russian accent but actually spoke in a vague mid-Atlantic one that might have been an attempt at stage British. As a nobleman, Mike was a total fraud, but he acted as if he believed it. We all played along.

Mike opened Romanoff's in 1941, at North Rodeo Drive, and by 1945 *Life* magazine had called him "the most wonderful liar in 20th-century U.S." Someone else would have sued, but Mike just smiled, and the customers kept coming, so much so that in 1951 he had to move to larger quarters at 240 South Rodeo Drive.

For Romanoff's décor Mike put on the imperial pretensions befitting a man known to his friends as "The Emperor." The place had a roof garden, a ballroom, a small private dining room, and the large dining room, which held twenty-four booths. The wallpaper was orange, green, and yellow. There were no secluded corners, and the entry had a short flight of stairs, situated so that everybody in the dining room could see who was coming in. Or, to put it another way, everybody coming into the dining room could make an entrance.

As you walked in, the first seven booths on the left were reserved. One was for the proprietor, who also favored his own food but seemed to prefer to eat alone, accompanied only by his two large dogs, Socrates and Confucius, whom I recall as being large bulldogs. If Mike liked you, or if you were a regular, you could hang around as long as you wanted. You could play gin rummy, some backgammon, or just talk. Mike put a premium on familiar faces, and if he didn't like you or if you were unfamiliar, you didn't have to do much to get kicked out. The place of honor was usually occupied by Humphrey Bogart—second booth on the left, as marked by a plaque, which also carried the names of Robert Benchley, Herbert Marshall, Sir Cedric Hardwicke, and a few others who were allowed to use it. Other Romanoff regulars were Jack Benny, Frank Sinatra, and Gary Cooper. Dinner regulars were Louis B. Mayer, Darryl Zanuck, and Harry Cohn.

Frank Sinatra was one of Romanoff's biggest fans—Frank liked to eat, and he had very good taste in food. The problem was that all those years of singing in nightclubs meant that Frank liked to eat at odd hours. He couldn't sing on a full stomach, so he got used to dining after his shows, very late at night. This would have been awkward for other people, except that other people tended to calibrate their clocks around Frank. When he was in the mood, Frank was also an excellent cook—mostly Italian. Frank would cook fine meals for special friends, and I had a lot of meals at his house with Spencer Tracy.

Another Romanoff's regular was Charles Feldman. Hollywood

Dean Martin, Prince Mike Romanoff, and Frank Sinatra having a good time.

was the home of great characters, and I don't mean great character actors. I mean people who really made the town work but who were not public in any sense—people who preferred to work quietly, out of the eye of publicity.

Agents, for example.

The cliché image of agents as cigar-chomping clods has an element of truth to it, but the broader truth was considerably more varied. Charles Feldman, known as the Jewish Clark Gable because he had the same hairstyle and mustache as Clark, happened to be my own agent. He was an elegant, dapper, unruffled man who always gave the impression that he had the upper hand in whatever negotiation he was engaged in—because he always did have the upper hand. He was also a gentleman who was reputed to have

Courtesy of Cathy Phillips

The legendary Hollywood agent Charles Feldman.

never won a game of gin yet never complained when he lost. A lot of Charlie's business was done over a table at Romanoff's. That way, even if the deal didn't work out, he was at least assured of a good meal.

Feldman was a hugely influential man in the history of Hollywood, but also one who has been underappreciated, because he preferred to work behind the scenes. I believe that Charlie invented what came to be known as the package deal. In the mid-thirties he realized that the problem with agenting was that you were effectively like a child raising its hand hoping that the teacher—the studio head—would call on you and hire your client. The balance of power was tipped entirely to the side of the studio head.

Feldman reasoned that the agents had to create some leverage for themselves, which he did by creating jobs for clients. He would take one of his own writers and have him develop either an original or adapted screenplay, for which Charlie would front the money himself. He would then cast the project with a couple of his own actors and finish off the package with one of his own directors. He would present the entire package to a studio, which could buy it at a hefty profit for Charlie but for less than it would have cost the studio to produce it themselves if it had to hire all the talents individually.

Because this took most of the work off the backs of the studios and the resulting picture would represent something of a bargain, a lot of studios went for the deal. And since Charlie had a premier group of clients—including John Wayne, Howard Hawks, Irene Dunne, Marlene Dietrich, and so forth—he could mix and match them in various enticing combinations. It was Charlie who put together *Red River* with Hawks and Wayne, for instance, although his name never appeared on the screen. The screenwriters for that independently made picture were also his clients, and Charlie even helped round up the money for it. Ditto *A Streetcar Named Desire*, although he took a producer's credit on that one.

By the time Charlie sold his agency in 1962, he was grossing around twelve million dollars a year. He produced a few more pictures and died, far too young, in 1968.

Charlie and the rest of the town liked Romanoff's because the food was special, often excellent. Mike flew in sole, and I remember an excellent charcoal-broiled steak for two, which was sliced and came with a very fine mustard sauce.

Mike specialized in French cuisine—he prepared a wonderful bouillabaisse, and a saddle of lamb as well. I also remember the steak tartare, the cracked crab, and the wonderful vegetables. Dessert was not for the faint of heart, or for anybody whose belt was on its first hole: cherries jubilee, crêpes suzette, and the house specialty: individual chocolate soufflés. Mike's banana shortcake was famous, and it deserved to be.

Mike was a great bon vivant. He always called me "The Cad," which has kept me laughing for more than sixty years. Mike's only real problem was that the expansion to South Rodeo became a challenge. The restaurant was simply too big—a lot of the time it looked underpopulated. Another problem was that Hollywood was, and is, always in flux—new people are always displacing the old, and those new folks want places of their own.

Romanoff's began to seem slightly old and musty, and Mike only made things worse by allowing his politics a place in the restaurant, actually distributing Republican campaign literature to his patrons. I don't care what your politics are, no one wants to be harangued over a meal.

The final nail in the coffin came when Mike opened a satellite restaurant in Palm Springs, ominously called Romanoff's on the Rocks. I was there for the opening of the new venture, along with Frank Sinatra and Jimmy Van Heusen, the songwriter whose real name was Chester Babcock and who was Frank's role model. Jimmy was a total original and an extremely funny man. He once called a bunch of apartments in a New York skyscraper and asked them to all put their lights on at an appointed hour. When they did, the name "JIMMY" was spelled out. Like I said, an original.

The restaurant was called Romanoff's on the Rocks because it was literally built into the rocks by Highway 111, just before you got to La Quinta. Mike gave the new place a lavish publicity send-off, but it failed. And that wasn't the worst of it: on New Year's Day 1962, he closed his signature restaurant on Rodeo Drive.

A day or so later Billy Wilder called Kurt, Romanoff's longtime maître d', and offered to support him in building his own restaurant, backed up by a group of other regulars—Jack Benny, Otto Preminger, and Jack Warner. Kurt opened the Bistro on Canon Drive, which thrived for years, and where he also served the individual chocolate soufflés.

So Romanoff's lived on, after a fashion. Unfortunately, Mike didn't. When his time came, Mike was in the hospital, being attended by his wife Gloria. Some doctors entered his room, looked at his charts, felt his pulse, mumbled something vague, and left. After they were gone, Mike said, "Chicken fuckers, all of them." He turned to Gloria and said, "Not you, my darling." And then he died.

Great last words.

I loved Romanoff's, and I loved Mike, but for me, judged strictly by the food, Chasen's was the best.

Why? Because Dave Chasen and his wife ran that place like a Swiss clock. Dave Chasen had been a vaudevillian, a dancer, a show business professional. His high point had probably been working as second banana to Joe Cook in *Fine and Dandy* in 1930, the first Broadway musical hit to have a score written by a woman, Kay Swift.

Dave's forte onstage was silence. He didn't speak, but became known for something called the "Idiot's Salute," which began with the sudden raising of both arms to his chin, as if to fend off a punch. As Frank Capra described it: "Then a sudden expression change from mock fright to the widest-eyed, most open-mouthed gargoylish smile ever seen on any face, followed by the right hand—fingers spread wide and palm toward viewer—crossed in front of his fixed idiot's smile like a slowly opening fan."

Dave was born in Odessa, Ukraine, and came to America when

he was still a toddler. He even appeared in a couple of movies in the early days of sound—*Rain or Shine* and *Old Man Rhythm*.

When things slowed up in his acting career, Dave opened Chasen's in 1936 with the financial backing of Harold Ross of *The New Yorker*. Ross's investment was three thousand dollars, and he was going strictly on the fact that he liked Chasen and had fond memories of the meals that Chasen had prepared for friends back in New York.

Chasen's started out as a glorified barbecue joint—the original name was Chasen's Southern Pit Barbecue—located on Beverly Boulevard, near Doheny. At this point Chasen's had six tables, a counter that seated eight, and a bar that sat six. The chili was twenty-five cents a bowl, the ribs thirty-five cents.

As soon as word got around, everybody who had known Dave, or eaten his food back east, began beating down the door. Within a year, Chasen's Southern Pit Barbecue had been transformed into a full-service restaurant. The menu underwent a serious expansion to more than thirty items, and Dave added a room with a couple of dozen tables. The staff grew from a total of three to dozens.

The mood at Chasen's was never particularly glamorous, but it was comfortable, clubby. Dave had very specific ways of doing things. For instance, Chasen's was the first restaurant I knew to have crushed ice in the urinals.

The regulars included W. C. Fields, Gene Fowler, Frank Capra, Nunnally Johnson, and, somewhat later, yours truly. Chasen's was my favorite restaurant from the time I was seven years old, when my father took me there shortly after we arrived in town. I loved the environment: dark wood, red leather booths, the pictures of celebrities on the walls. Then there were Pepe the bartender and Pierre the maître d', who made me feel part of the Chasen's family.

But mostly there was Dave and Maude Chasen. Dave was a small man, very energetic, and he had some of the comic's intrinsic manner—very upbeat, always with a joke—but he wasn't overbearing about it, as so many comics are.

Both he and Maude were attentive hosts who would walk around greeting the customers, and not just the celebrities. Their attitude was that if you had the good sense to eat at Chasen's, then you were as much a celebrity as any of the stars. That said, there were no walk-ins; you had to have a reservation. And Dave absolutely forbade autograph hunters, photographers, and gossip columnists. That's one of the reasons the patrons felt so relaxed—there was no possibility of saying or doing anything that would get in the papers.

Sometimes people would get up and do impromptu routines. Ray Bolger might perform one of his glorious eccentric dances, or Jimmy Cagney might sing a song entirely in Yiddish—he was fluent. Dave's best friend was probably Billy Grady, an old vaudeville chum who became head of casting at MGM, and therefore a very important personage. Grady had a special booth and was there most nights.

If Dave loved you, the restaurant was yours. When Dorothy Lamour was pregnant, she complained to Dave that she wasn't comfortable at Table 12 anymore, so he had a portion of the table sawed away to make room for her expanding stomach.

For Jimmy Stewart's bachelor party, Dave hired a valet to shadow Jimmy throughout the night. The valet fed him, wiped his chin, escorted him to the bathroom, and, for all I know, raised and lowered his zipper for him. Two midgets dressed in diapers were served on a silver platter. Bob Hope once rode a horse through the restaurant—I'll bet it was on a dare—and the character actor Charlie Butterworth once drove his Fiat into the place.

Dave once told me that Chasen's invented the Shirley Temple. It

The good life and good people at Chasen's. From left, Billy Grady, head of talent at MGM; Gloria Stewart; Jimmy Stewart; and Dave and Maude Chasen.

seems that Shirley and her parents were eating there when the little star got restless because her parents were drinking and she wanted to drink, too. The bartender threw together some grenadine, ginger ale, and some fruit, and served it to Fox's biggest star. Voilà!

By the time I was going to Chasen's regularly, Dave had added a sauna and a barber at the rear of the place, and there was also a Ping-Pong table—Clark Gable and Gary Cooper were regular players, as were W. C. Fields and Gregory La Cava. There was also a steam room on the second floor, and the men's room was furnished with reading lamps so that you could pass the time with the newspapers and magazines while you were answering nature's call.

By that time, the barbecue, which had always been Dave's special passion, had also been relegated to the rear of the building. But the food! Chasen's became famous for its legendary chili, but there was also Dave's hobo steak, which was cooked between inch-thick slabs of salt. Dave told me that he had learned the recipe from another comic in his vaudeville days, who had gotten the recipe from an actual hobo, which is why Dave called it the hobo steak. And then there was the cheese toast, and the fresh seafood served on pyramids of ice, and great desserts—strawberry shortcake, wonderful apple pie. And I particularly remember the banana shortcake with chocolate sauce.

When Dave died in 1973, Jimmy Stewart was on location, but he left the movie and came back to Los Angeles to deliver the eulogy. Frankly, anybody who knew Dave would have done the same. After Dave's death, Maude kept the restaurant going for a long time, but eventually it got too hard to keep it up. When the place finally closed in 1995, a friend of mine bought the picture of me that Dave had kept in his office, and gave it to me.

I still have that picture. That, and my memories of Dave, Maude, their wonderful food, and, most important, their friendship.

Along with Chasen's, Natalie's and my favorite restaurant was La Scala, which was run by Jean Leon, who got the seed money from a tip given him by Frank Sinatra. Jean ran a superb eating establishment, but his real passion was wine—his ambition was to have his own vineyard, which he eventually realized. Not surprisingly, Jean's wine was as good as his food. As with Chasen's, La Scala was a no-press zone; there were never any stories in the paper about who had eaten there the night before.

Jean proved his friendship for me a hundred times, not just emotionally, but financially. When jobs were scarce and I was having trouble making ends meet, Jean ran a tab and carried me. Years later, when my life and career had both turned around, Natalie and I invested in a new venture of Jean's, Au Petit Jean, along with the

Getty Images

Restaurateurs David Chasen and Mike Romanoff with Humphrey Bogart during a Christmas Eve party at Bogart's house in Beverly Hills.

director George Stevens—a good man, if a trifle remote. Au Petit Jean was successful for a while, and then it wasn't. Finally, it closed. But as far as I'm concerned, Jean Leon was much more than a great restaurateur; he was a great friend.

Another legendary restaurant was in the Ambassador Hotel on Wilshire Boulevard. The hotel itself opened in 1921, on the site of a dairy farm on top of a small hill. At the time, there wasn't a whole lot else on Wilshire. The hotel's original purpose was as an all-inclusive winter resort for Eastern and Midwestern families who wanted to escape the cold, much like the Breakers in Palm Beach, which opened a few years later. The resort had more than twenty acres, and featured riding trails, golf courses, and views of the mountains and of the ocean. The Ambassador had a great clientele, because Hollywood didn't really have another first-class hotel until late in the 1920s. Scott and Zelda Fitzgerald and Winston Churchill all stayed there.

Within the Ambassador was the famous Cocoanut Grove, which seated a thousand and was decorated with artificial palm trees supposedly recycled from the set of Valentino's movie *The Sheik*. The story goes that the Grove had a maître d' named Jimmy Manos, who was a friend of Valentino's, which enabled the Grove to get the palms for little more than the cost of trucking them away. Over the years the place added papier-mâché coconuts and toy monkeys whose eyes lit up.

It sounds like an outlandish urban legend, but it's tragically true. The first time I went to the Grove, I spent most of the evening craning my neck looking at the monkeys.

It seemed to be a stylish idea at the time.

For the generation just before mine, the Grove was a key site—Mack Sennett discovered Bing Crosby while he was performing there, and Joan Crawford won so many of its dance contests that she became the unofficial Charleston champion of Hollywood.

The chef at the Grove, Henri, was French. He was heavy on local ingredients like avocados, grapefruit, and asparagus, as well as abalone, sand dabs, and little California oysters, which you could order either raw or cooked. The hotel became a familiar setting in the movies; you can glimpse it in the Judy Garland version of *A Star Is Born*, and the Art Deco entrance appears in the Jean Harlow film *Bombshell*.

The odd thing is that, for all the fame of the Cocoanut Grove itself, the Ambassador Hotel was never all that financially successful. In the 1950s Paul Williams was hired to do a makeover, and the

Bettmann/CORBIS

Virginia Bruce, Cliff Edwards, Clarence Brown, Nancy Dover, and their party
ring in the new year at the Cocoanut Grove in LA.

irony was that Williams, who had designed a lot of fine homes in
Beverly Hills and Bel Air—not to mention the Beverly Hills
Hotel—would probably not have been able to get a room there be-
cause he was African American.

The 1964 movie *The Best Man*, with Henry Fonda, has quite a
few scenes photographed at the Ambassador, notably the lobby and
other public areas. The good times for the hotel permanently ended
when Robert Kennedy was assassinated in its kitchen in 1968. The
Ambassador, and the Grove, limped on until the hotel finally closed
in 1989. It stood derelict for years, the roof of its ballroom sagging
under the weight of leaks and its lush gardens becoming wild.
Eventually the place was demolished.

A hotel that has had a considerably luckier life is the Chateau

Marmont, off Sunset Boulevard. The Norman-inspired Chateau opened in 1927 at the height of the era of Hollywood excess, and it's still there, bearing the slightly worn aura of the place where Jean Harlow honeymooned with cameraman Hal Rosson, where the young Howard Hughes entertained his ladies before moving over to the Beverly Hills Hotel.

For Europeans who had come to Hollywood in the wake of war, the culinary scene was grim. When the Viennese Paul Henreid arrived in 1940, he observed that "there was terrible food, with one or two exceptions"—those being Romanoff's, Perino's, and Chasen's. "That was about it. Those were the three places you could go and get a decent meal."

Perino's, which opened on Wilshire Boulevard, was spawned by people who had worked at Victor Hugo. It was more than just upscale—it was *swanky*. Alexander Perino was the kind of guy who trained other restaurateurs—he once claimed that eighteen Los Angeles restaurants had been created by his protégés, and it's certainly possible.

Perino's didn't subscribe to any of the gimmicks that some of the other restaurants did. The mood was conservative and the service was excellent—not by the standards of Hollywood, but by the standards of Paris or London. You wore your best to Perino's—not just clothes, but jewelry as well—because it wasn't the sort of place where you ordered a hamburger. Alex imported twenty-four-inch-square linen napkins from Ireland, and had a rigid ratio of one waiter for every eight diners to ensure a high level of service.

At Perino's the bill of fare included dishes like salmon in aspic

The ultra-upscale Perino's restaurant.

and tangerine soufflé. As Paul Henreid observed: "They would have something that was then unheard of, like a crêpe filled with lobster or with crab." Perino's served a lot of Italian dishes—some pretty fancy, such as polenta or gnocchi—and lots of fresh fish, especially Dover sole and sand dabs. Alex insisted on homemade brown stock and fresh tomato puree for even a basic Bolognese sauce. Oddly for an Italian gentleman, Alex wouldn't cook with garlic, which he detested. And he wouldn't refrigerate his tomatoes, because he believed it destroyed their flavor.

It was a very chic restaurant, strictly white-glove, and was favored by business types and political movers and shakers—Los Angeles people more than Hollywood people. Frankly, Perino's was always a bit snobbish for me, but then, it didn't really cater to the movie crowd the way, for instance, Chasen's did.

Alex sold the restaurant in 1969, and it kept going for a number of years before closing in the late 1980s, as so many of the once great LA restaurants did. We shot at least one episode of *Hart to Hart* there, and I don't know if we would have been able to do that while Alex was running the place; while he tolerated movie people, whom he probably regarded as nouveau riche, he might not have wanted an actual film crew in his restaurant.

I don't know if the Players would be considered a great restaurant, but it was certainly a great experience. The Players was owned and run by Preston Sturges, the great writer-director of such flamboyant farces as *The Palm Beach Story* and *The Miracle of Morgan's Creek*. Opened in 1940, it became very popular during the war years. The Players was an old wedding chapel at 8225 Sunset, slightly west of the Chateau Marmont. Sturges converted the chapel at great expense into a three-level entertainment and dining complex. The idea was that you could have a fine meal, then go downstairs and take in a play. When the play ended, Sturges could push a button and the floor leveled out to become a supper club with an orchestra on a revolving stage.

A lot of the actors who starred in Sturges's movies went there, as well as Humphrey Bogart, Charlie Chaplin, Orson Welles, Willy and Talli Wyler, and—when he was in Hollywood working on a script for Howard Hawks—William Faulkner. Sturges was there

The exterior facade of The Players restaurant. To the right is the Chateau Marmont.

most nights holding court, and sometimes Howard Hughes would join him.

Sturges ran the place like an indulgent uncle. There was a barber shop on the mezzanine level, and if he felt like entertaining some of his close friends, he would close the place for a private party without warning.

The food was excellent. The menu included some French dishes, turkey croquettes, and canapés, and a lot of drinks that Sturges named himself, although he reputedly drank only old-fashioneds.

Sturges comped his friends, and was always coming up with inventions that were expensive and of dubious worth—like tables that swiveled out to provide easy access. He once made plans to build a helicopter pad in the parking lot so that he could take delivery of fish that were still flopping, but the neighbors protested, and it never happened.

In his quiet moments Sturges may have silently counted out how much it was costing him every week to run the place, but since he was Preston Sturges—a profligate personality if ever there was one—I doubt it. However brilliant, he was erratic and a terrible businessman. He poured hundreds of thousands of dollars into the Players until the IRS took it over in 1953.

As the 1940s turned into the 1950s, the Hollywood dining experience on the whole became far more sophisticated. And after the war, as stars began venturing out from Hollywood toward independent production, Europe was no longer just a place for vacations. It followed that Hollywood restaurants began to adopt what their patrons found palatable in countries overseas.

I remember Scandia with particular affection, because the food was so tasty. Scandia was on Sunset Boulevard from the time it opened in 1946, and it kept going until 1989. Early on Scandia cooked primarily brasserie food, more than slightly Germanic—pot roast, brisket, stuffed cabbage, boiled beef with horseradish sauce. Peter Lorre was there every Saturday, and other regulars included Gary Cooper, Ingrid Bergman, Rita Hayworth, and Marilyn Monroe.

Over the years the menu evolved and began featuring more sophisticated dishes, including a gravlax appetizer that had a spectacular mustard dill sauce. Kenneth Hansen, who was the chef and ran the place, would make occasional trips to Scandinavia and bring back new recipes. He also arranged for seafood from the North Atlantic to be flown in year-round.

Time + Life Pictures/Getty Images

A couple uses binoculars to read a distant wall menu at Scandia restaurant.

Christmas was a special time at Scandia, as Ken would offer authentic Norwegian holiday foods—notably roast goose stuffed with apples and prunes. Actually, it was almost always a special time at Scandia. Ken reserved the bar there, the Viking's Club, for his favorite customers, or just important ones. And yes, I was there a fair amount of the time. Sometimes at the Viking's Club people would hit the aquavit just a little too hard and fall off their bar stools. Literally.

I also frequented a place called the Cock 'n Bull, which was just down the street from Scandia, and where the best customer was probably Jack Webb. The Cock 'n Bull had a terrific Sunday brunch that was a big deal and hard to get into. The Moscow Mule was invented there: ginger beer, vodka, and lime in a copper mug. Terrific restaurant, good drink. Jack Webb was a good man with a bottle, but he wisely steered clear of the Moscow Mule in favor of scotch.

Also in that neighborhood was a place called Alan Dale's, which was known for carrying actors on the cuff during thin times, including one named Wagner. Alan was a special man, especially to me.

Ken sold Scandia in 1978, and it closed eleven years later. His timing was excellent, because the great years of Scandia corresponded to the period when the town got more adventurous with its dining. During that time people were open not only to experimentation, but even to gimmicks. That hunger for novelty led to places like Bit of Sweden, which was on Sunset near Doheny and introduced the smorgasbord to Southern California, and Don the Beachcomber's, founded by a guy whose name wasn't Don and who wasn't a beachcomber.

Ernest Raymond Beaumont-Gantt liked to serve rum drinks at

a bar in a Hollywood hotel and somehow became known as Don the Beachcomber. He opened the first glorified tiki bar/restaurant in 1937, on McCadden Place in the heart of Hollywood. He actually changed his name legally to Don the Beachcomber.

Don's was a totally stage-managed environment, a bunch of cozy little rooms united by concept and by craft. Regularly scheduled artificial rainstorms would make an appropriately romantic sound on the corrugated iron roof. The artificiality extended to the outside. Don's was surrounded by a lush stand of bamboo and was accordingly hard to find, unless you knew to look for a miniature bamboo forest; even the signage was tough to read.

The place was a riot of Polynesian kitsch—palm trees, coconuts, shells, carved wooden gods, sharks' teeth. There was also a shop that sold rum and leis. The tables were made out of varnished woods and were arranged in such a way that you felt you were on a secluded little island. The rooms meandered and had names such as the Black Hole of Calcutta and the Cannibal Room.

Every so often there would be a bunch of bananas hanging off a pole, and if you wanted one you could simply pluck it and eat it. Needless to say, the illumination was dim, mostly by candles, which made—in the worst case—every woman look mysterious or—in the best case—beautiful.

Don had been a bartender, and a bartender he remained, devising rum drinks that would knock you on your ass. The most lethal concoction I remember was something called the Zombie, invented for a customer who was nursing a vicious hangover and who'd begged Don for some hair of the dog. Don took one ounce apiece from six different rums, combined them with what he claimed were secret ingredients, and poured it all into a tall, slender glass.

The next time the customer came in, Don inquired as to the

effectiveness of the drink, and the man said he had no idea—"It made a zombie of me." From then on, any customer requesting the Zombie was limited to two, and I have no idea how anyone could drink that many.

Other drinks that Don invented were the Vicious Virgin, the Never Say Die, the Cobra's Fang, the Shark's Tooth, and the Pi Yi, which was served in a miniature pineapple. The food that Don served was a variation on Chinese, exotically so, a far cry from what was offered by the chop suey joints that constituted Chinese food at the time. Don used ingredients like oyster sauce and water chestnuts, and the first time I had Mandarin duck was at his restaurant.

Don's desserts were in line with his entrées. He became famous for something he called a Snow Cake, which I recall being a mound of shaved ice covered with pieces of fresh pineapple and candied kumquats.

Don the Beachcomber's broadened the palate of the movie colony considerably, and it was such a hit that it became a small chain. The maître d' in the Hollywood restaurant, Roy Bradley, later ran the Palm Springs Don's, and the chain expanded as far east as Chicago. The original place was torn down in 1987, long after the vogue for Polynesian-themed restaurants had vanished.

I have a very special connection to Don the Beachcomber's, one that probably only another actor could appreciate. In 1949 I made my first film, *The Happy Years*, which was directed by William Wellman. Despite his terrible reputation around town—they didn't call him "Wild Bill" for nothing—he was very kind to an extremely green kid.

When I got the check for my performance—it was for seventy-six dollars—I cashed it and took my parents to dinner at Don the

Beachcomber's in Hollywood. For my mother, who had always believed in me and my ambitions to be an actor, that dinner was a
confirmation of her instincts about her only son; for my father, who
thought my aspirations were crazy, the dinner was a marker that
maybe he had been wrong, and that maybe his kid's instincts deserved some respect.

So, you see, there are very good reasons why I still remember the
Mandarin duck. And, God help me, the Zombie.

I had that check framed and mounted on Natalie's and my boat.
After the tragedy, I put everything from the boat into storage, until
the Northridge earthquake destroyed the storage facility. Gone, all
gone.

Several long-lasting restaurants started out at about the same time
as the Players, including La Rue, which had several reasons for its
popularity:

1. The food was considered quite good.
2. If you showed up there, you'd probably get a mention
   in the *Hollywood Reporter.*

The reason was that Billy Wilkerson owned the restaurant, and
was usually found at Table 1. Billy plugged the place relentlessly in
the pages of his not exactly objective trade paper.

I've mentioned earlier that Billy owned both Ciro's and the Trocadero. Deeply self-destructive, he had a habit of selling out successful enterprises for no good reason other than that he was bored with
them. The gamble was in designing and opening the operation; once

it was successful, Billy would lose interest and move on to another high-stakes risk.

One of his earliest projects had been the Vendôme, at 6666 Sunset, just across the street from the *Reporter*'s offices. He opened the place in May 1933, which took some courage—the Depression was at its worst. The Vendôme was supposed to be a gourmet grocery and specialty store—supplies from Fortnum & Mason for the English colony, Westphalian hams, caviar, that sort of thing. But in order to maximize the number of customers who came through the door, Wilkerson decided to serve lunch as well, and the Vendôme quickly became nearly as important a spot as the Brown Derby. The lunch crowd at Vendôme might feature Mae West, Joan Crawford, Clark Gable, perhaps Marlene Dietrich. It was at Vendôme that Louella Parsons nabbed what she always regarded as the greatest scoop of her career—when Mary Pickford told her she was divorcing Douglas Fairbanks.

After the Trocadero opened in 1934, Billy had the wind at his back. He opened Ciro's in 1940 and then, in 1945, La Rue, with a chef who had run the Italian Pavilion at the 1939 World's Fair in New York. Despite the provenance of its head chef, La Rue was mostly French, or at least French in style—one of La Rue's specialties was spaghetti served in a large silver tureen. It was especially popular for its Tournedos La Rue, made with white truffles, which I remember with some affection.

Bogart liked La Rue, and the first booth was informally called Bogart's Booth; the booths were golden leather. There were two huge chandeliers hanging over the dining room. Supposedly, cleaning their crystals was such a difficult task that it had to be performed by specialists from San Francisco.

For all of Billy's love of suave surroundings, he himself was a workaholic, and in such constant motion that he rarely had time for a good meal. Left to his own devices, he would eat canned sardines on toast or deviled egg sandwiches. Women were possessions, and I was told he preferred his French poodles to any of his five wives—by no means an unusual conclusion for men who have five wives.

Billy was a moving target—the only property he ever really held on to was the *Hollywood Reporter*—and he sold off La Rue only five years after opening it. The place kept going until 1969.

Billy had two reasons for going into the nightclub business. One was his firm belief that most Hollywood dining places were "pedestrian." They lacked glamour, and they lacked sophistication. (Billy was a habitué of Paris and its pleasures.)

And the other reason was that restaurants and nightclubs deal mostly in cash, and Billy needed a lot of cash, for Billy was a gambler. All of his activities, from running the *Hollywood Reporter* to his restaurants, were essentially sideshows compared to his gambling.

Typically, he'd cram all of his work into the mornings and head for the racetrack in the afternoon. Most days, he'd gamble at Hollywood Park, but there were also regular visits to Santa Anita. He carried a pair of dice in his pocket, and a deck of cards was always nearby. If Billy was at a restaurant, he'd roll the dice to determine who picked up the check, and on Fridays he would take the company payroll and stake it all at the track.

Billy was a regular at the private poker games that were held weekly at either Sam Goldwyn's or Joe Schenck's house, where only very high rollers were allowed, for the simple reason that the chips cost twenty thousand dollars apiece. (Other players were Jack Warner, Carl Laemmle Jr., and David Selznick.)

How bad was Billy? In 1936, he borrowed seventy-five thousand dollars from Joe Schenck to convert a small hotel on the French Riviera into a casino. Two weeks later, he phoned Schenck and told him he had blown all the money at the casino at Monte Carlo within days of his arrival.

Most years, his gambling losses would average around a hundred fifty thousand dollars, but in the first six months of 1944, he hit a cold streak during which he lost almost a million dollars. Business bills went unpaid, and vendors began shipping material to Billy COD. During one particularly dicey period, Billy wasn't able to pay his losses at the poker games at Schenck's or Goldwyn's. His response was to barter advertising for his gambling debts.

Billy survived only because of the generosity of his friends, and the cash flow provided by his restaurants. Between Ciro's, The Trocadero, La Rue, and the *Hollywood Reporter*, Billy grossed about a million dollars a year. After expenses, he was left with about a quarter million dollars. A normal human being could have lived quite nicely within that, even allowing for bad runs at the track or the casinos, but Billy was not a normal human being.

Finally Joe Schenck told him that if he was going to gamble that kind of money, he had to own the casino. Joe Schenck's words struck a chord, and Billy began planning the Flamingo Hotel and Casino in Las Vegas. He eventually get euchred out of it by Bugsy Siegel and the mob, but the original impetus behind the Flamingo was Billy's.

At one time or another, Billy also owned the Sunset House and L'Aiglon. He also supposedly installed illegal gambling at Arrowhead Springs. They were all landmarks of their time, yet Billy Wilkerson, one of the great characters who circled the movie business for forty years, is almost forgotten today.

*

All these restaurants were famous to one degree or another, but I
also think with fondness about a couple of places that haven't been
much written about—the Tam O'Shanter, for instance, which is
still in the Los Feliz district, where it was built in 1922 by the great
art director Harry Oliver (who designed the original *Seventh
Heaven*) as a fairy-tale Norman inn. The interior is a series of fairly
small rooms, some with roaring fireplaces and walls decorated with
tartans and family crests. It's another example of the restaurant as
movie set, and all the better for it.

The Tam was one of Walt Disney's favorite restaurants, probably
because it was close to his studio, and Disney was too much of a
workaholic to travel long distances for a good meal. The Tam has
always served good food, and it's now the oldest restaurant in Los
Angeles in its original location.

Then there's the Smoke House, built across the street from Warner Bros. in 1946. It's Tudor Revival in style, but the interior is all
red leather and heavy timbers—a very masculine atmosphere. Because of its proximity to Warner, the Smoke House has always been
popular within the industry and has been the site of wrap parties
for several generations. Today George Clooney has a plaque on his
favorite booth, just as Bogart did at Romanoff's.

The Café Swiss on North Rodeo Drive was a pleasant and
mostly casual place, popular with the émigré community because it
had a European feel—the proprietors were Fred and Laura Hug,
both Swiss—as well as a strong musical orientation. It became one
of the hangouts for the town's composers and arrangers.

Joe Marino, a pianist who worked at both Paramount and MGM
and was Kay Thompson's accompanist, played the piano most

nights, and a lot of his pals were regulars. Said pals included Johnny
Mercer, Harry Warren, Ned Washington, Conrad Salinger, Sammy
Cahn, Kay Thompson herself, and Jimmy Van Heusen. Joe was a
good friend for a lot of years.

I always enjoyed eating on the patio there, especially for lunch.
In the 1950s Gable went there a lot, usually alone, eating a corned
beef sandwich while reading the paper. Walter Winchell liked the
place as well. In later years, Jack Lemmon, the great German director Fritz Lang, and Natalie and I were all there a fair amount of the
time.

The food at the Café Swiss had a foot in both Continental and
American camps. You could get a great veal cordon bleu there, or
just a solid sandwich. Fred Hug ran the kitchen for more than
thirty years, until he died; Laura kept the place going for a few
more years, but the Café Swiss finally closed in 1985.

There were other Mitteleuropa places—the Hofbrau Gardens
on Sunset near Vine for years featured a ceiling covered with tree
branches and birdhouses and strung with lights, so you could imagine you were in a Bavarian beer garden.

A little further down the scale was the Tick Tock, which was
located on North Cahuenga for more than fifty years. Technically,
it was called the Tick Tock Tea Room, and it was well known for
serving big portions at modest prices. If money was tight, you could
have lunch at the Tick Tock and you would be able to skip dinner.

The Tick Tock was so named because, when it opened in 1930,
owner Arthur Johnson installed an old wall clock. One clock gradually led to others, and by the time the place closed in the late 1980s
there were clocks everyplace you looked—dozens and dozens of
them.

Another place for the average Joe was Schwab's Pharmacy, on

Sunset Boulevard, right on the edge of the Strip. (Actually, there were six Schwab's around town, but when people referred to it, they meant the one on Sunset.) You didn't have to be an out-of-work actor to eat at Schwab's, although it helped.

Schwab's served eggs and onions, lox and bagels, as well as steaks. If the Schwab brothers (Leon, Martin, Bernard, and Jack) liked you, you could run a tab. If they really liked you, they'd cash your checks at midnight or make a delivery to Malibu. There was a sign near the counter that read "Coffee 40 cents per cup. Maximum 30 minutes." Nobody paid any attention to the second half of the sign; people hung around for hours.

Then there was—and is—Nate 'n Al's, a classic deli that has catered a lot of parties, including a lot of mine. Frank Sinatra would be there occasionally, but mostly the clientele were great Jewish entertainers of an earlier generation: Groucho Marx, George Burns, George Jessel.

Nice people, nice place. But then, you could say that about the town itself.

Good-bye to All That

The 1950s are usually regarded with nostalgia, but for Hollywood it was far from the best of times. There was the Red Scare, which began in the late 1940s and lasted for ten years. There was the competition from television, which helped drop weekly movie attendance from ninety million in 1946 to forty-six million in 1952, with a commensurate drop in profits. At my studio, 20th Century Fox, the profits dropped from $22 million in 1946 to $4.2 million in 1951.

Then there was the order from the Justice Department that forced the studios to divest themselves of their theater chains, depriving them of what amounted to a financial floor for their films. The Justice Department wanted to put an end to what it saw as a monopoly and bring about a more open system of production and exhibition. It achieved that goal, as independent producers like the Mirisch brothers and small studios like American International achieved far more success in the 1950s and 1960s than they ever could have before. But this was accompanied by unintended consequences as well—stars turned producers, and the results could be mixed both artistically and financially.

More crucially, the newly spawned independent producers made more and more of their pictures in Europe in order to save money in the face of unionized Hollywood wages. Studio space and personnel in Italian studios were quite inexpensive compared to Hollywood, and the favorable exchange rate made them even more attractive.

If it hadn't been for television, Hollywood would have become a ghost town by 1960.

All this meant that the studios dropped older, expensive stars in favor of younger, inexpensive ones. Gable left MGM; Ty Power left Fox. Production plummeted. By 1959, the studios that had made forty, fifty, or even sixty pictures each year in the 1930s were now making twenty-three (MGM), eighteen (Warner Bros.), or a bottom-of-the barrel eleven (Universal).

Because there were fewer and fewer pictures being made, there was less and less work. And there was a changing of the guard. Clark Gable died in 1960, Gary Cooper a year later. The great stars who remained, such as Jimmy Stewart and Fred Astaire, went where the work was, so Hollywood gradually began to feel depopulated.

Lots of actors slowly migrated to television as a matter of survival, as did writers and actors and crew. If you hooked on to a successful TV show, you were guaranteed thirty-nine weeks of work a year, which by then was something only top stars could hope to have in the movies.

All this began to have a distinct effect on Hollywood. If the 1930s had been a slow turning away from the vast mansions that the stars and producers of the 1920s had built, that process became even more advanced by the 1950s. Blue jeans replaced tuxedos. James Dean rented a little house in Hollywood to go along with his apartment in New York, and he would have laughed in your face if you had suggested he buy a house in Bel Air.

As the business began shifting, became less about Hollywood and more about other centers of production, I got out of my Fox contract. What ended it for me was when the studio asked me to accept second billing to Elvis Presley in *Flaming Star*. Colonel Tom Parker made sure that no other actor in a Presley picture got any attention at all, because they had no lines at all. I decided to head for Rome, where a lot of interesting movies were being made.

I've spent a lot of time here talking about place, about ambience, but I have to be honest—when I think of those days, I think mostly of people.

Bob and Sally Cobb. Mike and Gloria Romanoff. Dave and Maude Chasen. J. Stanley Anderson. Jim Cagney. Jimmy Stewart. Spencer Tracy. Clifton Webb. Laurence Olivier. Billy Wilder. Barbara Stanwyck.

Some of these people were actors, some restaurateurs, some entrepreneurs. But they were all men and women who could warm your hands just by being around them.

There are very few places left in town that have the wonderful charm that attracts a traditionalist like myself. Even the Bel Air Hotel has changed. Today, there are a few places that still maintain the old vibe: L'Ami Louis in Paris, La Grenouille in New York, and the wonderful Charles Masson and his family, whom I love.

But things change. It's the way of the world. I guess that's why nobody writes letters anymore.

Ethics have deteriorated in business in general. Start with the government and go down . . . It's so hard to teach values: looking someone in the eye, shaking hands, not being litigious, being grateful for the bounty that life so often gives us. Lawyers have taken over the country, as have the insurance companies and lobbyists in general. When I was brought up, a man's word was his bond. Pensions are disappearing, with a resultant loss of security. An interconnected social system that lasted for close to a hundred years is breaking down.

I grew up in a different time. I don't mean to imply that it was necessarily perfect. But I think we can all agree that it's become far more difficult to move through life with some sense of balance, not to mention integrity. Technology has altered values in a way that makes it hard to have any intimacy. And most damaging is the fact that the level of vitriol is off the charts.

Many people my age believe that the films have grown old, lost their power to enchant. Sometimes that happens to people. If you fall in love with the movies when you are young—I think the critical ages are around eight to fifteen or so—by the time a half century has gone by, the movies are bound to have changed a great deal, because it's their nature to appeal to the young, who attend more frequently than the old.

For example: 1965 is generally thought of as a good year for Hollywood, on the cusp of the great changeover from old to new. Old masters like Ford, Wilder, and Wyler were still in the game, and exciting young talents like Arthur Penn, Sidney Lumet, Blake Edwards, and John Frankenheimer were beginning to make waves.

That year, the wonderful old director Raoul Walsh talked to Hedda Hopper about how Hollywood had changed. According to Walsh, it was all for the worse: "Cooper, Gable, Flynn—all gone at once—it's left a big hole. The Academy Awards are now a joke—a songwriter's holiday. It's 'What song can we get him or her to sing?'

This used to be a place out of the Arabian nights in earlier times—now the so-called stars go around dressed like bums—in old jeans. It's unbelievable."

Change the names of the recently deceased, and you could imagine the same speech being given by any number of the unwilling retired actors, directors, or reporters of today pining for the golden age of 1965.

But even amid an occasional complaint, I remain optimistic. The movies have always been about passion, enthusiasm. Those qualities were reflected in all aspects of our lives, both in the movies we made and the lives we led. In most meaningful ways, they still are, and the best films continue to reflect them. *The Artist* was a movie that transcended period and caught the joyous essence of the movies, as well as the emotionally volatile temperament of the people who make them.

It won Oscars for Best Picture, Best Actor, and Best Director, and it did my heart good.

Films are often compared to dreams—I call them eyelid movies—and watching a movie is a lot like being in a dream state, but, surprisingly, I've never dreamed about them. For decades I've had one recurring dream that never varies. It's about Sonny, the good-natured horse with splashes of paint on his shoulder that I worked with when I was a boy.

In the dream I'm with my father. Sonny is old, and we're taking him back to his breeder, to return him to the pasture where he was bred and to say good-bye. When we get to the pasture, Sonny is already there, but he's someplace where I can't see him. I'm upset because I haven't actually said good-bye to him, and I need to do that.

I set out for the pasture to find Sonny, but before I start walking, I turn around and look back at the place I came from. There I see my family—my daughters, my grandchildren, all the people I've loved, some of whom I've loved and lost—people I hope and believe I will see again someday. At this point in my dream, I always feel a comforting rush of gratitude for everything I'm leaving behind. And then I set off to find Sonny.

It's at this point that I wake up. In the dream I never find Sonny, but that doesn't bother me. One day my dream will eventually have the perfect happy ending that so seldom happens in life. An ending . . . just like in the movies.

Diana Cammarano

Acknowledgments

My memory for my own life is thankfully excellent, but there was a lot of history going on in Hollywood before I got here nearly eighty years ago. Besides all the wonderful stories told to me by older friends who were there at the time, I consulted a number of books on the subject. Among the most valuable were *Hollywood: The First Hundred Years* by Bruce Torrence, *Out with the Stars* by Jim Heimann, and *Gone Hollywood* by Christopher Finch and Linda Rosenkrantz.

I'd like to thank Mort Janklow—a legend in the literary world, and for good reasons—he's incredibly smart, enthusiastic, and most important, wise—the consummate agent. He immediately saw the potential of *You Must Remember This*. Rick Kot at Viking edited the book with creative style and grace, and Nick Bromley and all the people at Viking have put the pieces together in a beautiful package. Elizabeth Applegate has been with me for thirty-seven years, through good times and bad, and never faltered. She found pictures of my childhood that I wasn't even sure I had.

Finally, I want to thank Scott Eyman, my esteemed literary collaborator. Scott's knowledge of and love for the movies and the industry that produces them is unparalleled, but that's probably not as important as the fact that writing two books together has bonded us in a deep and valued friendship.

And to all of you who have watched me over the years—my life would not have been possible without you. Thank you.

Index

Page numbers in italics refer to photos.